BUCKLEY!

Lord of the Crackerbox Palace

*The Incredible Story of the First **HIP***

Comedian

By

William J. Millman

SB

Sunset Beach Press

SB

Sunset Beach Press

ABOUT LORD BUCKLEY

"*'The Nazz,'* which I consider a classic...(is) like nothing I have ever heard before in any language... If you had access to the pulpit, you would undoubtedly make converts by the millions. You haven't a single rival I can think of."

-HENRY MILLER, Author

"He was hysterically ahead of his time – you walked out talking to yourself."

-LARRY STORCH, Actor

"My God, he was great."

-MILTON BERLE, Entertainer

"A man for people who loved comedy at its best and most original."

-REDD FOXX, Entertainer

"Perhaps the most magnetic performer I've ever met."

-STUART WHITMAN, Actor

"He's my favorite comedian."

-GEORGE HARRISON, Ex-Beatle

"The most unforgettable character I've ever met."

-SCOTT BRADY, Actor

"I never knew the heights of my profession until I met Buckley."

-DEL CLOSE, Second City Director

"He was a visionary."

-ROBERT MITCHUM, Actor

"Every time he'd go on stage, there was a bit of electricity crackling from him to the audience...(he) was a great 'pro,' who brought a lot of happiness to the world."

-ED SULLIVAN, Columnist, TV Host

TO LADY LIZBETH

And All Members of The Royal Court –

Past, Present and To Come

THE PIED PIPER
(EXCERPT)

The following excerpt concludes Lord Buckley's translation of the Pied Piper of Hamlin, and is spoken by a young crippled boy who has followed the Piper and the town's children to the outskirts of town.

...."For He was, He was,

He was jazz hipping us, he said,

To a reallll, crazy, JOYOUS land,

Close at tone and near at hand

Where soda pop rivers gushed

And hot dog trees grew,

And flowers, flowers,

Flowers blew to a perfumed hue

And everything, everything was so cuckoo and new,

And sparrows lived brighter there than peacocks here,

And dogs drag-raced with the leaping deer,

And honeybees swung with wondrous kisses
instead of stings,

And circus ponies were donned with eagle wings,

And just as I solid knew

That my bent frame would be straight,

The sweet jazz stopped and I stood still

And dug myself - OUTSIDE...

Mmmmmm, at the world's gate,

Playing the loner against my will,

With my bent frame limping as before,

And to never pick up

On that sweet jazz no more.

Hey Jack, hey Jack!

Let's you and me be watching

The scores up of all men, especially pipers.

If they make pipers free from jazz, rock and roll,

Or the 'Blue Suede Shoes,'

Yehhh Jack, let's solid keep our promises...

And we'll never blow the blues.

No, we'll never, never blow the blues

PROLOGUE

Los Angeles – 1959

The anxious chatter stopped abruptly.

Onstage, dressed in his customary tux and tails, a cigarette dangling from his hand, Lord Richard Buckley entered regally from the wings and was striding toward the microphone with an appraising glance to the audience.

The five-piece jazz group behind him played a cool flourish as he stepped to the mike. Applause sounded loudly, with a few boisterous shouts of greeting: "Buckley!" "Your Lordship!"

Standing rigidly erect, shoulders back, head held high, he seemed even larger than his 6'1" frame, possessed of an energy, a vitality, a presence that captivated the audience with its sheer magnificence. Over three hundred people... hypnotized.

A brilliant spotlight highlighted the curl of his moustache, his strong, resolute jaw, even a few shadings of grey in his closely-cropped black hair. He seemed proud, aristocratic, and alive.

Ringsiders might have detected a slight redness to his eyes, edged by a wrinkle or two, but the impression of a handsome, vital, magnetic personality was inescapable.

And then there was the voice.

"M' Lords and M' Ladies," he intoned with a deep, clear, sophisticated British accent. "M' Lords and M' Ladies of this Royal Court, you are truly a divine audience."

He commanded their attention even as he thanked them for giving it. They responded with total, respectful, anticipating quiet. Coughs were suppressed, sneezes squelched, unnecessary conversation eliminated.

"I should like to explain to you," he began, "that in the Royal Court of Lord Buckley, all ladies and gentlemen are Lords and Ladies... So may I have the pleasure of saying: Good evening, Your Majesties."

As yet unaccustomed to their new-found royalty, many in the audience shook their heads in disbelief; some giggled; most applauded his sagacity. Members of the band watched and waited, smiles spread across their faces in anticipation. They were well-aware of the fantasy trip His Lordship would soon be orchestrating, and were anticipating the journey even more so knowing that Buckley would be using their *jazz language* to create his own hip future-world. Buckley took a drag from his cigarette and continued, his words an ever-changing tide of inflection, stress, and volume.

"You see, I believe in the nobility of the gentility, Your Highnesses. You are no longer at the world's finest nightclub, but at Church – the Church of the Theater."

Suddenly, as though transformed by his own words, the sound of his speech changed drastically.

"So you see," he said with the smooth coolness of jazz, his voice picking up the sound and rhythm of a hip black musician, "I'd just like to welcome all you cats and kitties to the High Mass of Hip."

Aware from the quizzical expressions and decades of experience that not everyone was "pickin' up on what he was layin' down," His Highness took time to explain in his audience's language. "The semantic of the hip," he told them, "arose from the intimate social language of the American beauty Negro." With the care of a loving father, and the power and intensity of John Barrymore, he revealed "the great power" of the semantic: "The zig-zag semantic was contrived in this first action movement by the slaves, many years ago, when they wished to discuss things they didn't want the *mahster* to get hip to. That's why it was called hip talk.

"We should like to use this delicious semantic, which has two fantastic powers: it'll take anything from as far back as you can reach, and... whaaaamp... bring it up to the fence of now, over the fence of now, and on the pad advance a thought of the newest meaning in the volume of sound.

"Then it is insured and diviniated by the flexibility and beauty of the American Beauty Negro humor." As Buckley spoke, his compassion for the Black experience sounded in his love tones and sparkled in his knowing eyes.

"For the Negroes, there are many banks. And one of the great banks is the bank of compensation, for the divine, beautiful, warm, sweet, swinging American Negroes had to laugh at so many things, for so long, that were not funny. As a consequence, they deepened the wells of their humor, until it sparkles with a beauty that makes it endless in its depth and sacred in its clarity. And when this particular type of semantic is applied, as to this salute to your fancy, and is done in truth, properly applied, some strange and wonderful things happen.

"I would like to demonstrate these powers by doing a dash of William Shakespeare, which in hip would be..," his voice lowered and then rose to a sweet riff as it musically replied, *"Willie the Shake."*

"Do you know why they call him Willie the Shake?" he asked, only to be met by questioning looks tinged with smiles. "Because he SHOOK... everybody!" he roared, and in that instant the audience sat upright in their seats and Buckley was off and running.

"Hipsters, Flipsters, and finger-popping Daddies... Knock me your lobes," began his hip translation of Antony's speech at the funeral of Caesar. At first, he waited for the reaction, pausing with great restraint to allow the belly laughs to wash over him. Then, fueled by their precious energy and excited by the caress of their laughter, he rolled faster and faster, firing off salvos of words and phrases with a tantalizing jazz rhythm that demanded close attention and intense concentration.

Some people could stay with him, transported by the tempo, the facial expressions, the fluctuating volumes, and accents. Others, though mystified by the sincerity of his tone and the magic of his creation, lost the razor-sharp edge of his meaning and followed by instinct only.

Behind his stirring renditions of *The Gettysburg Address* and several other jazz translations, the band played a soft gasser of an accompaniment while an attractive young woman sang melancholy snatches of the blues. As Buckley moved from one piece to another, improvising between licks and jamming off random happenings, he took a drag off his cigarette and watched his audience – giving and receiving vibrations at all times.

"Would it embarrass you, if I told you I love you?" he asked, and they knew he did.

Up and down and around he lifted them, twirled them, spun their lives this way and that to show them a side of their world – or themselves – they might have never seen but for his interpretation. For two hours he brought them laughter, sadness, outrage, and freedom while he entertained them, with such great tact they never realized all they'd absorbed, and with such fervor they never forgot. During those two hours they stepped out of their mundane existence into the vision of the most Royal of Bohemians. Old falsehoods were examined in a new light and revealed in all their baseness. Life was given new meaning; thought was carried to a higher plane. He spoke of Truth, and he spoke with love in his heart for the people – *all* the people. Finally, seemingly all too soon, it was time to go.

"M' Lords and M' Ladies of the Royal Court," he said, his British accent returning, "I would like to tell you, in all significance, that your gracious cooperation and the wonderful feeling of your presence and understanding here, to those of us up on the stage this evening, only goes to prove, more and more.... that the Flowers, the beautiful, mystic, multi-colored flowers, are not the flowers of life. That people... people are the true flowers of life, and it has been a most refreshing pleasure for us to have temporarily strolled in the garden of your attention. God swing you, and God love you."

To the wave of applause and the cheers for more, be bowed his head ever so slightly and spoke with a sense of joy and gratitude: "Thank you. Thank you all very, very much."

They stayed, clapping, whistling and cheering, until he was gone and it was obvious he would not return. Then they left slowly, as if dazed, their conversations carrying a hint of excitement, wonder and pride, their minds busily evaluating and absorbing the stimulating input.

For the people in that audience became lords and ladies that night, and they carried the joy and honor of that moment locked in their hearts for a long time thereafter.

They had witnessed one of Lord Richard Buckley's finest performances, the culmination of nearly forty incredible years in showbusiness. From the mining camps of northern California to the finest theaters and clubs of New York and Chicago, from the Roaring Twenties to the frantic Fifties, Buckley cut a swath through this nation that will never be forgotten by those lucky enough to have experienced him. He carved out a path to the future, in which a new breed of thinkers who would come decades later would understand the messages and philosophy he was laying down.

And yet, in less than a year, he would be dead, caught up in a tragic snarl of legal, professional, and personal problems. He lived as though tomorrow might never come, and squeezed more life into his 54 years than most men ever dreamed. He was a comedian, an emcee, a television personality, a gracious conman, a film actor, a father, a visionary, and a preacher. But most of all he was a real person, striving to entertain and motivate others while living a life of joy, experimentation, and love.

A rare, extraordinary human being – that was the Lord of Crackerbox Palace.

That was His Most Royal Highness, Lord Buckley.

CHAPTER 1

Northern California – 1911

The streets of Tuolumne were choked with dust.
Etched by miners' wagons and pounded by the horses young
cowboys galloped through town, the roadways resembled
nothing so much as wide paths of brown talc as small clouds
erupted with every step and spun out from beneath whirling
wheels.

Dick Buckley, five years old, and his older sister Nell,
played in the shade to avoid the shimmering intensity of the
dry summer heat. The two youngsters, dressed in raggedy
hand-me-downs, were an inseparable pair, with Dick always
concocting some crazy new adventure and Nell always willing
to back him up.

The slow, rhythmic walk of tired work horses coming
into town caught Dick's attention, and he quickly prepared
his sister for their favorite pastime – serenading the local
ranch hands with two-part harmonies and bedazzling them
with fancy footwork. As three young cowboys and their

exhausted mounts came into view, Dick stepped boldly out
into the street and raised his hand for them to halt.

"Stop in the name of the law!" he announced to the
surprised cowboys. "We're gonna entertain you guys and
you'll never hear anything like it. It's gonna cost you – but
you'll love it!"

While the hands looked at each other in bemused
amazement, Dick and Nell launched into one of the more
popular songs of the day – like a bouncy "*Everybody's Doing It*"
– or even a tune of Dick's own creation. The two youngsters
sang their hearts out, and when they finished Dick stepped
proudly forward. "Pretty great, huh?" Confronted by his
expectant gaze, the three young men tossed some coins into
the thick dust and rode off laughing at the daring of the two
small-fries. As soon as they were gone, Dick and Nell
scrambled in the dust, sifting through the fine brown powder
to find their booty.

Sometimes the Carlotta Mine whistle would blow
before they had time to search out their hard-earned treasure.
If so, fearful the screaming signal marked the coming of the
devil – as their mother, Annie Laurie, had told them – they
marked the spot with a rock or stick and rushed immediately
back home. Since Annie was unwilling to physically punish
her children, she sometimes used fantasies to frighten them
into minding her, so when the noon whistle blew she knew

they'd soon come scurrying home for lunch. Only after they'd gulped down their food did they return to find their reward.

For nearly a year, Nell claimed the lion's share of their profits, having convinced Dick that since nickels were larger than dimes, they were worth more. When Buckley finally realized the deceit, he took out after his sister wielding a knife and chased her all over the neighborhood. When Nell finally decided to make her stand, Dick stabbed her in the hand, drawing a tiny drop of blood. Outraged by his attack, Nell ran home and showed her mother the wound, which she had squeezed to make it bleed more dramatically.

When Annie Laurie asked her how it had happened, Nell replied, "I cheated Dick."

Unsympathetic, Annie said, "Good for Richard. He should have cut you from ear to ear. We don't need any cheating Buckleys." As punishment, for the next week Nell had to eat dinner on the back porch with the dog.

Tuolumne was that kind of town. Tough, demanding. It was a typical California mining town, with tales of riches and gold fever contrasted with the abject poverty of most townspeople. But it was all part of America's dream, and people made-do with very little, waiting patiently for their opportunity to come. They were poor, but strong of character and courage.

For Buckley's parents the dream was no different, and survival was a constant struggle every day of their lives. Lord Buckley's father was the oldest of fourteen children born in the late 1800s to a wealthy Englishman who owned a race track in Manchester, England. One day, young William, then 28, tired of donating his coppers to the Church, rebelled against his father's strict upbringing and decided to stow away on a ship to America, to find fame and fortune. It wasn't long before he was discovered onboard, however, and made to work his way to San Francisco.

Even as his ship was crossing the Atlantic, a young divorced mother of two was working in a San Francisco laundry for $1.50 a day, sending all the money home to her mother who was caring for the two infants. Annie Laurie Liddel was her name, an attractive but somewhat untidy woman whose path was soon to cross that of William Buckley.

When William docked in San Francisco, Annie Laurie happened to be there at the wharf, and a chance meeting evolved quickly into love. William was a tall, handsome, immaculate man, while Annie could be expected to have her slip showing and her hair disheveled; but the magic was there. He asked her to marry him, and she accepted. He got a job so that he could buy her new material for her wedding dress and be married in style. Though appearances were not especially important to Annie, she allowed friends to style her hair and arrange her gown, and her wedding picture reflects her beauty and joy. Having saved for the occasion, the happy couple went to the finest hotel in the city for their wedding night, and feasted on a 35-cent dinner.

After the wedding they moved to Auburn, where William became foreman of a mine, and together they ran a miners' boarding house. They had a Chinese cook, and Annie made lunches to feed their tenants on the job. It wasn't long before five little Buckley's came on the scene, with little Nell the youngest at the time. Early one winter's morning, Nellie being barely two years old, the miners got up and dressed the children as was their custom. The first miner up had to take a shovel and clear a path through the sixteen-foot snow drifts to the outhouse so the men could empty their slop cans. One morning before his shift, William noticed a few of the miners entertaining themselves by tossing Nell into the huge snowdrifts. Although she loved it, her father took her aside and taught her to say "Goddamn son of a bitch" so that whenever he wasn't there she could shock anyone who might mess with her and make them leave her alone. Barely able to speak, Nell was rewarded with gold stars to motivate her to say the phrase more clearly. Before long, she had a star-studded crib. The next time the miners grabbed her to toss her into the snow, they were so stunned to hear this little child shout "You Goddamn son of a bitch!" that they left her alone while her father chuckled quietly off to the side.

That winter was an especially tough one, with much too much snow, and Annie was pregnant with what was to be her last child. The weather was so bad the doctor could not get up to the mine, since the snow would ball up in the horses' hooves and make it impossible for them to climb. So Annie made the trek down the mountain wearing her snowshoes, with all the children in tow, and had her baby, Richard Myrle Buckley, in Tuolumne. When Dick was born on April 6, 1906, he was the last of six children and the eighth child in the household: Bob and Elsie (from the previous marriage), Mabel, Lester, Ben, Jim, and Nell. "He was the eighth child when seven was already too many," Nell remembers. "And such a big child: he weighed 14 pounds at birth! But everyone loved him anyway. He showed such adult initiative as a child. He was independent, didn't need anybody to show him a good time – he was always in the lead." At six years old he sang *"The Tea Kettle Song"* in the school Christmas play – a natural performer. The teacher worried about him remembering his lines, so she sat behind the curtain to give cues. Not only did Dick remember all his lines as he raised his little eyebrows and blinked his baby browns, but he managed to flirt with the teacher while he performed. He was always happy. Always talking. Always telling the other kids how to do whatever they got into.

"He was the boss. He created a world for them."

But good humor was barely enough to get by. The vicissitudes of the mining business made it difficult for William to support his large family. So he was forced to leave on frequent money-making trips that lasted up to two years at a time, working anywhere he could, to send home $40 a month to help the family get by. Annie took in laundry and ironing to make ends meet. The family existed on "beans, green tomatoes, and tomato chow-chow."

In William's absence, all hell broke loose. Dick Buckley's birth nearly coincided with the great San Francisco earthquake, and from his early youth people remarked about cause and effect. Unfortunately for Annie, most of the other children were just as uproarious. Whether they were cheering the dog and coyote fights that rocked the saloon, or riding bareback on mine burros around the tiny one-room schoolhouse – whooping like incensed Indian raiders – the Buckleys made Tuolumne an eventful place for its 200 residents. Their bottomless sense of humor gave birth to innumerable pranks and earned them a reputation of infamy with their neighbors.

In an attempt to protect them from their own outgoing exuberance, the children were repeatedly warned to

stay away from drunks, but were instructed that if they ever
saw a tramp with a blanket folded neatly over his shoulder (in
the fashion of bedrolls at the time) they were to run home as
fast as they could. One day a stranger appeared in town with
a neat blanket-roll, but he wasn't dressed at all like a tramp.
He had spit-shined boots and creases in his pants, not a speck
of dust anywhere. He walked up to Dick and Nell, who were
playing in the streets, and showed a big toothy grin. With a
look of uncertain recognition, he asked Dick, "Are you a
Buckley?"

"None of your damn business," Dick replied, his lip
curled in scorn, "and we're going home 'cause you're a tramp
and my mother doesn't want tramps around here." So the two
kids took off and ran home, to their $10/month house with
most of the windows broken out. They never used the gate,
but instead ran around back, ducked through a hole in the
fence and ran up the three stairs to confront their mother.
"What's the matter?" she asked anxiously as they came sliding
to a halt.

"There's a drunk coming!" they shouted.

"Is that so? What does he look like?" she asked. Just
then she saw her Will, as she called him, smiling as he came
through the same hole in the fence. The children ran out the
back door and ran around to the front, but when they got to
the front door they saw the tramp kissing their mother!

Thinking that the stranger was forcing himself on Annie, the two kids attacked him, swearing, scratching, even chewing on his pants. "It's okay children, it's your father," Annie consoled. "Go out and play." The children stopped, stared for an instant, and followed their mother's order. As Dick walked past his father, Will reached out and patted his head as he laughed. "That's my boy."

Buckley was good at making people laugh. One old lady, Mary Seagrit, was notorious for hating children; her dogs were trained to attack even the smallest tykes. Dick considered her a challenge, to "make that old son of a bitch smile." So one afternoon, accompanied by his sister, he purposely walked in front of her house knowing the old spinster was sitting on her porch.

"Good morning," he said with a big bow as he doffed his hat. "I'm the world's greatest guy, and I love you."

The woman took one look at him, and then at his somewhat dubious sister, and burst out laughing. He'd won her affection.

The next day, Nell tried to duplicate her brother's feat. Repeating every phase of Dick's delivery, especially the tip of the hat and a bow, she was met by an icy glare and a mumbled, "Oh Christ." She had failed miserably, and was furious at not getting the adoration her brother received. But the magic was Dick's, and his alone.

Though life was a continual struggle in Tuolumne, it was at Christmas time that the Buckleys' lack of money became most painfully obvious. While other children regularly expected some sort of gift, Dick and Nell had learned to go without. Much greater was their surprise, then, when one Christmas season their older and more pious sister Mabel came home from Church with the news that any children who were good and came to church for three weeks before Christmas would get a present of their choice.

For twenty-one consecutive days the two little kids managed to control their instinctive behavior and even attend mass. The family was shocked to see the two ragamuffins taking their baths every night without a fuss, and combing their hair on their own. They even seemed to enjoy it! They really wanted their presents. So it was with a great deal of pride, and no small amount of anticipation, that they came to Church on Christmas Day, scrubbed, neat, and thankful.

After the ceremony was almost complete, however, and the other children had been given their gifts, it became evident that Mabel had made a mistake: it had been the parents who were supposed to buy the gifts. The minister, seeing the dilemma, offered them a piece of fruit to compensate for their disappointment. Dick exploded.

"You son of a bitch!" he shouted, jumping up at his place, tears in his eyes. "You lied to us!"

The minister moved quickly to eject them from his church, grabbing each by the ear. However, he had badly underestimated their displeasure and moxie. Responding to the cleric's tug, Dick proceeded to punch the minister in the stomach while Nell followed suit by biting him on the leg. The scuffle continued right out the door, with the children ejected into the street. It was a wiser and humbler clergyman who returned to the pulpit.

Poor Mable was so embarrassed, she cried all the way home. She thought she'd never be able to face the congregation again. In fact, she had to be reassured by fellow church-members that everything was ok for her to come back before she returned. Cousins Ann and Mat were so upset for the children, they put their pennies together and made sure their Christmas wish came true.

After such a monumental let-down, it's not surprising that Dick and his sister were left with a bad taste in their mouths; they returned to their previous ways with a vengeance, and never looked back. As Nell described it in her later years: "I started out a Methodist, and now I'm a Heathen."

As if life in the dreary mining town wasn't bad enough, tragedy struck the Buckleys repeatedly. Annie's oldest son, Bob, who had followed Will into the mines and was supplying a little extra income for the family, was killed in a

freak accident. One evening, when he was just 19, Bob was
riding up from the depths in a mine elevator with several of
his fellow miners, exchanging jokes and insults, when a burst
of laughter sent his head arching backward. A beam struck
him across the forehead, and he died immediately.

Then, in 1914, William returned to Tuolumne for the
last time. He had miners' consumption, for which there was
no cure, and he'd come home to die. His cheeks would flush
a bright red and he had difficulty getting out of bed –
sometimes he couldn't even make it to the dinner table and
the family had to hand-feed him. Sitting beside his bed in the
small room, the children took turns fanning him to combat
his fever, but they hated the task. For their mother spared
them the realization and grief of a death that was inevitable,
and so the kids thought Will was just exaggerating his illness,
having no understanding of the gravity of the situation. Annie
Laurie refused to allow the children to be hurt when there
was nothing that they could do about it, so she kept the grief
to herself and maintained an optimistic facade.

Unfamiliar with their father, and not really knowing
what to do with him, the children resented the discipline he
enforced for the first time in their lives. They couldn't wait
for him to get better and leave again. Nell would ask, "When
is that man going to leave?" and Annie Laurie would just
smile sadly and answer, "It won't be long."

The children were used to telling their mother to "go to hell," and having a free run in the house, doing pretty much exactly what they wanted. But with Will home it was something else indeed. One night, as they were about to have supper, Nell was sassing her mother fiercely when Will reached over and whacked her across the mouth with a large cooking spoon, chipping a tooth. Nell never spoke out of turn again until after her father died.

As his illness worsened, William discussed his funeral plans with Annie. Because money was so scarce, he told her there was to be no hearse; he'd made arrangements with friends to carry the casket down the hill to the graveyard. He insisted on a plain pine box because he didn't want the older boys – Ben and Jim – to have to pay for his funeral for the rest of their lives. At the time they were working as apprentices for 75-cents an hour.

Sitting close to him on the bed, Annie told him not to worry, that she had taken out a $1000 life insurance policy which she'd paid for with money she saved from her washing and ironing. Amazed at her strength and foresight, Will regretted on his death bed that he hadn't found a job in the local mills and stayed closer to his family.

Annie Laurie stayed with Will as much as she could during his final days, comforting him as best she was able. But finally, his condition worsened, his breathing became shallower and more labored, and he died. The younger children were kept unaware of their father's death, and when the mortician came to the house and prepared the body for viewing in the front room, the kids were told not to enter the room because Will was sleeping. They were just pleased they didn't have to fan him anymore.

The day of the funeral the family rode in a rented surrey, while Will was carried to his rest by friends and family. The younger kids were simply told that they were going on a picnic, and Nell was even allowed to wear a new hat. But when she tipped it at a woman from town and was received by laughter, she cussed out the unsuspecting woman in no uncertain terms. Annie Laurie scolded her and forbade any further hat-tipping, but Dick suggested, "By God, if she wants to tip her hat, let her!" There was no more tipping of the hat that day, however.

With Will gone, Annie Laurie returned to her washing and ironing to support the family, with only infrequent interruptions in her grueling schedule. One such break came when friends of the family invited Annie and Dick, her youngest, to the San Francisco Exposition of 1916. Dick was dressed immaculately in a homemade Little Lord Fauntleroy outfit, and was warned to keep clean until their neighbors came by to pick them up.

Completely captivated by his sparkling duds, Dick strutted proudly around the weather-beaten house until the novelty of his dressy outfit ran thin. Then, directed by whatever it is that unerringly guides a youngster to the one spot he should avoid at all costs, Dick found himself down at the stables, frisky and ready for fun. After a good roll in the manure, and even a brief dip in a water trough, Buckley answered his mother's call with well-deserved apprehension. A brisk whippin' with a brush was his just reward.

The whipping hurt Annie more than her son. Even as the spanking continued, Dick laughed aloud and swore his imperviousness to pain: "I don't give a goddamn, go ahead." With such unspectacular results, the beating stopped shortly, he was washed and dried, and they finally set off for the Exposition.

Thousands of people crammed the fairgrounds, and Buckley was enthralled by the hustle and bustle of a totally alien world. So carried away did be become, that he wandered off from his mother and their friends to investigate on his own – and promptly got lost.

Not one to panic in such a remarkable situation, Dick wandered around for quite a while with one eye on the exhibits and one on the lookout for someone he recognized. A policeman finally spotted him walking coolly amongst the multitude, neither excited nor distressed. The officer asked the youngster if he was lost, and was stunned to receive a lecture from the ten-year- old on the responsibilities of the police to prevent children from getting lost at big fairs. Somewhat taken aback, the policeman hurriedly searched out Annie Laurie and returned the ice-cream and candy surfeited Dick to his mother, leaving the officer with an ill-concealed look of confusion. Returning to Tuolumne, Annie Laurie found life even more intolerable than before. Living in a $5/month hut, she realized the family had to move elsewhere, namely to the "Big City" where the boys could make good money as apprentices in a manufacturing company. Annie went on ahead to Stockton with the larger part of their meager belongings, and Ben, Nell and Dicky followed by train.

Having ridden the train to the Exposition, Dick was the expert in rail travel; Nell and Ben had never been on a train and so looked to their younger brother for guidance. The three kids brought the last remnants of their family possessions with them, including a large gilded birdcage. They didn't own a bird, but they refused to leave something that beautiful and precious behind.

The boys dressed as well as they could, with Nell in her stocking cap and best dress, but even their best wasn't very impressive and they "looked like quite a circus" as they got onboard carrying their bundles and empty canning jars stuffed into the bird cage. They piled everything on the upper racks, ignoring the curious stares of the other passengers.

Suggesting "I'm a man of travel, you'd better do as I say," Dick demanded absolute attention to his every command, and both Ben and Nell sat ready to move at a moment's notice. After a couple of stops, which Dick inspected carefully through the windows, he told them to get ready to get off and ordered them to pull all their stuff down from the racks. Just as they were all set to get off, Dick told them to put everything back – it was just a joke! Ben threatened to kill Dick when they got to Stockton for his tomfoolery, but until then they were at his mercy.

Dick had them jumping up and down for about three stops, loading and unloading, with everyone laughing at their predicament. Ben and Nell were furious and embarrassed, but they were afraid not to do what he said for fear they'd miss their stop.

At long last they arrived in the teeming metropolis (to them it was like New York), and were greeted by a friend of the family. Dick scurried off the train in a big hurry, but Ben's long legs were right behind him. He chased Dick all around the depot, caught him and delivered his retribution. Despite the unfortunate conclusion of his prank, Dick loved every minute of it.

The family moved into an $18/month house that turned out to be a little too expensive, so they moved again to a $10/month palace that was "just right for a family to beat up – and we were the family to do it," according to Nell. Dick was so enthusiastic about his new home that he carved his initials – "R.B." – into the front door.

Dick quickly became the neighborhood hell-raiser, leading all the kids around at play and instigating more than his share of mischief. Dick took after his mother, who had "the sweetest line of bull you'd ever want to hear," but Dick wasn't bashful about using his gift of gab to his own advantage, while Annie reserved her talent for storytelling.

It wasn't too long after the move to Stockton that Annie's luck took a turn for the better, and a semblance of order returned once more to the Buckley household. An old sweetheart by the name of Al Harlan brought that change with him, when he fell in love with Annie after a chance encounter reunited them. An iceman by trade, whose mother had been kidnapped by the Jesse James Gang, Harlan always carried a gun with him – just in case the gang should return. He had known Annie years earlier, but had been forbidden to see her when her father learned of Al's pistol-packin' proclivity.

Their love renewed, a short courtship brought a man back into the Buckley family dynamic. Al was a kind, hardworking, dependable man who quickly won the hearts of the entire gang with his sunny disposition and well-considered philosophy of life amidst the chaos. "I'll never tell your boys what to do," he'd tell Annie, "but I'll set 'em an example and protect the girls when it's needed."

Often exhausted after a long day of hauling blocks of ice, Harlan would still remember to bring Annie bouquets on special occasions; most likely they'd just be a hefty section of flowering bush he'd picked up on the way home. No matter. The sincerity of his intentions and his goodness of heart won him unprecedented attention from the children: they massaged his feet, fetched his slippers, and even tempered their exuberance whenever possible. Annie flourished too, and the group of them were extremely close, for the first time as a complete family.

Dick grew quickly as the years passed, and he was a good-sized young man by the time he dropped out of school in the eighth grade. His grades had been good, and he was a voracious reader, but he decided his time could be better spent by helping Al deliver ice during the days and educating himself by reading whenever he found the time. Of course, his self-education faced stiff competition from his outside interests: mainly having a good time.

He hot-wired his father's prize auto, given to him by stepson Lester, and drove it wildly throughout the surrounding area at night to impress his bevy of girlfriends. An unrepentant daredevil, he put the car through a torture test of thrill-seeking maneuvers, eventually flattening all four tires.

At 16, he spent a short time as an apprentice cabinet maker, but gave it up after deciding he preferred "to hammer blondes" rather than cabinets. Another short stint as a 'choker setter' in a lumber camp followed his return to ice delivery, but that too proved unsuitable.

Having mastered the ukulele, and possessed with an extraordinary voice and set of lungs, Buckley thought his fellow workers would be pleased when he took time out to entertain them with a large repertoire of songs. Unfortunately, dressed in his argyle socks and knickers, the lumberjacks looked upon him as a "goddamn sissy" and made life difficult for him.

Dick accepted their irritation with a smile. He was big, strong, well-coordinated and bright. The world was his to enjoy, and the more they complained about him, the more he baited them. Climbing to the top of a tree in just seconds, he'd spit down on the lumberjacks and call them every name in his extensive book. His practical jokes were legendary, and feared. But good looks and a ready laugh couldn't ingratiate him with men who had made up their minds, and he eventually moved on.

Dick was bored with his surroundings, and eager to get out to see the world he'd only read about. Always the adventurer at heart, he was quick to accept an invitation from his brother Lester to visit him in Texas. Lester was working in the oil industry there, and he convinced Dick that he could make good money working the fields.

"I was on my way to Mexico, to join my brother in an oil campaign," Buckley recalled, "and I got as far as Galveston, Texas, where I met with a long angular Texan in a boarding house playing guitar. The first date I ever played in my life, and the first theater I ever was in in my life was the million-dollar Aztec theater in San Antonio. The manager of the theater, Mr. Epstein, he said, 'Gentlemen, I'm paying you, I want to pay you, but, you're the lousiest act I've ever booked in my life,' (Buckley laughed fondly and warmly) 'AND he was right!"

His Lordship's career had begun.

CHAPTER 2

With such an auspicious beginning, it's not surprising that the Duo did not remain intact long. They struggled their way north and east, eventually landing in New York where their incompetence became glaringly apparent in the brilliant spotlights of the Great White Way. After six months of total failure, culminating with a short stint eating "swell swill" out of garbage bins, Buckley packed up his ukulele and set off on his own.

Temporarily nonplussed by his East Coast experience, Dick returned to the West Coast and San Francisco, where he and his brother Jim lived the wild, chaotic life of Twenties bachelors. The   practical jokes continued, their love lives flourished, and Dick gained invaluable experience working small clubs throughout the Bay area.

It was a wonderful time for a person of courage and motivation, a time of changing styles, philosophies, and mores. As F. Scott Fitzgerald put it, "all faiths in man were shaken."

The Twenties were a time of youthful rebellion, Prohibition and speakeasies, dance marathons, flagpole sitters, "talkie" motion pictures, and jazz. Babe Ruth, Douglas Fairbanks, Charles Lindbergh, and Al Capone were the biggest names of the day; cynicism was the national call word. "What most distinguishes the generation (since WWI)," said Walter Lippmann, "is not their rebellion against the religion and the moral code of their parents, but their disillusionment with their own rebellion."

In this chaotic, exciting atmosphere, Dick Buckley was at the forefront of experimentation and change. In New York, he had been exposed to crazy new music, wild women, and outrageous ideas. In San Francisco, he developed his own version of this lifestyle, complete with bootleg booze, big cars, and plenty of adoring women.

By 1927, however, one lady in particular had captured his eye. Emerald Botting, a wealthy woman some years his senior, became the first Mrs. Buckley, and the newlyweds moved into an apartment not too far from the *Golden Gate Theater* where Dick appeared for three months in 1928. The foundation for his later career was constructed at this time, as Dick emceed the variety shows as well as singing an occasional song himself. His carefully groomed spike moustache and mother- of-pearl cigarette holder evoked the image of genteel civility that was to become His Lordship's trademark.

Another trademark were the wild parties. At one of his classic get-togethers, Buckley surreptitiously nailed the windows shut before his guests arrived and then built a roaring fire in the fireplace "so that they wouldn't catch a chill." As the temperature soared and sweat began to trickle down the cheeks of the meticulously coiffed and gowned ladies, Dick apologized for the "stuck" windows and began to subtly suggest that everyone disrobe to cool things down a bit. As the alcohol flowed and Dick became more and more persuasive, the party took the turn he had orchestrated and was wailing right along when a knock penetrated the boisterous scene.

Dick motioned for everyone to keep the noise down while he went to answer. As he swung open the door, an elderly lady from the next apartment stared in shocked disbelief to see Buckley standing erect and proud before her wearing only spats, garters, and socks.

"Oh, Mr. Buckley!" she stammered, before fleeing in terror; the party-goers roared with laughter and the festivities continued.

Money was plentiful during this time, as Dick was paid $750 a week at the *Golden Gate*. Incredibly, Buckley lived from paycheck to paycheck, spending his money as quickly as he received it: on parties, clothes, booze, and to support a small cliche of 'friends' who were not doing as well as he. He also sent money home every week to his mother - about $25 - addressed to "My Sweet- heart." When other members of the family asked Annie Laurie why Dick didn't stay home and take care of her himself, she'd answer, "How many of you would ever send me $100 a month to put in the bank, so I could be free in my home and buy all of you Christmas presents?" Some family members would criticize Dick when he wasn't there, but when he came home, they couldn't get close enough to him. "He loved everybody," Nell said.

Under the stress of this wild existence, his marriage never stood a chance. When he finally closed at the *Gate* in late 1928, Dick looked eastward once again for new audiences to conquer. Aside from New York, only one city stood out as something special: Chicago.

A wide-open metropolis of big-time gangs and unlimited opportunity, the Windy City had become the unchallenged entertainment mecca of Mid-America. Organized crime – headed by Al Capone – possessed millions of dollars that were freely invested in every form of 'entertainment' – from prostitution and gambling to speakeasy nightclubs. The proliferation of small clubs, as well as the growing popularity of dance marathons, required a host of new entertainers: singers, dancers, and above all, emcees.

Of the latter, Dick Buckley was probably the very best. A superb all-around performer, Dick's strongest assets were a quick, spontaneous wit, and an incomparable ability to command attention.

Arriving in Chicago on February 15, 1929, Dick was immediately impressed by the attention paid to gangland leader Capone; just the day before, in a garage on the North Side, Capone's hired killers had eliminated Bugs Moran's henchmen in an ambush of machinegun fire. The Saint Valentine's Day Massacre it was called, and the murders quickly hipped Buckley to who was really running the show in Chi-town.

Fast talk and some impressive clippings from San Francisco got Dick represented by the Bert Levy Agency, and soon he was working gigs at $150/week. At a party after one such appearance, Dick was introduced to Alfred E. Painter, an early impresario of the wildly popular Walkathons – grueling tests of stamina in which the last contestants standing won. Dashingly handsome, glib, and charismatic, Buckley impressed Painter immediately and was signed on as one of seven emcees.

For several months Dick worked with the Painter organization, often appearing in shows housed in large circus tents erected at the end of the street car lines. The money was good, the audiences large, and Buckley quickly developed a following of near-fanatic followers – many of whom were women.

The sudden, shocking failure of America's financial and business institutions stunned the nation and brought the Great Depression crashing down upon its unprepared citizens. Thirteen million people were unemployed – nearly 25% of the total work force. Food lines stretched for blocks; wandering hoboes numbered over one million.

But for Dick, the Crash produced quite a different atmosphere. Whereas the dance marathons had been a popular form of entertainment since the mid-20's, danceathons and walkathons became a way of existence for many young people in the 30's, and a staple of showbusiness across the country.

A grueling and yet highly-entertaining business, walkathons combined long-term endurance competition with Vaudeville to create a unique hybrid that drew spectators by the thousands. Contestants vied to see who could continue moving on the dance floor longest, with contests lasting as long as three months – with the walkers moving continually the entire time except for short rest spells!

Overseeing this spectacle, and contributing humor, songs, skits, and patter, were the irrepressible emcees, whose job it was to keep the entertainment level as high as that of the competition. Grocery auctions, mock arguments, even weddings were constantly arranged to keep the customers satisfied. Down on the dance floor, the competitors were occasionally called upon to sing a song or demonstrate some fancy stepping, and the audience threw money to show their appreciation. Some of the best dancers would be sponsored by local businesses, and they wore mini-billboards while they competed – for $40/week.

The short breaks didn't allow any time for fancy dining, so the contestants ate 6-8 small meals each day. Of course, they needed the energy, to meet challenges such as the 15-minute races used to eliminate couples after several thousand hours of competition. As the walkathons became better established and organized, the sites changed from tents to huge auditoriums, such as the 6500-seat Coliseum in Chicago. It was in these massive halls, throughout the country, that Buckley perfected the talents and skills that were to last his lifetime. He would sing, tell jokes, do imper-sonations, (most notably of Amos and Andy), burlesque anyone, and most importantly, attract every eye in the auditorium whenever he chose.

"He was the most dynamic entertainer in the walkathons," said fellow-emcee Rajah Bergman, and that included such luminaries-to-be as Red Skelton and Milton Berle. "They would entertain people for months at a time: all hours of the night they would keep people entertained. The contestants were very well taken care of, and were well-aware that they had to look pressed and cleaned at all times; even their sleeping quarters were well-cleaned. We dragged people from their radios and gave them hilarious comedy during the Depression days. We originated comedy sketches, blackouts, doing different shows nightly – since we were playing for the same people all the time. "We had successful contests that the local movie theater owners did not like; they fought us in the courts of every state but not on the issue of cleanliness...

"The walkathons were in direct competition with the theaters, because you could come in for a quarter and stay all night, see live entertainment, and you never knew what kind of excitement they were going to dream up next. The acts had to be outrageous in order to compete with the theaters."

Rajah recounts an incident that demonstrates Buckley's incredible appeal. "The first time I came to Chicago, I went to the apartment house where all the walkathon performers

lived. I got talking with the manager of the place – he knew
everyone – and told him I'd come to town to emcee the
shows. 'Good luck,' he told me, 'the people aren't going to go
for it. They want Buckley.'

"Well, I had heard of this Buckley, but I knew he
wasn't in town, so I auditioned for the job and got it.
Opening night, I come out, and I have it arranged where I
pretend to be a contestant in the audience and my straight
man calls me up on stage.

"So he calls me up, we do our schtick, and then he
introduces me. Instead of applause, what do I get but 5000
people chanting 'We want Buckley!' at the top of their lungs.
Over and over: 'We want Buckley!' They wouldn't stop, so
finally I picked up the rhythm and led the chant. They finally
got tired and let me continue, but I've never seen a crowd
that devoted to anybody."

With the walkathons a national phenomenon, a cross-
country circuit developed including nearly every major city
from coast to coast. As the top emcee on the circuit, Dick
Buckley was in heavy demand by all the competing
promoters, including Leo Seltzer – the man who was later to
popularize the roller derby.

In 1931, Buckley was persuaded to join the Seltzer
troupe, and with a retinue of some forty regular participants

he toured the country delighting tens of thousands of fans in dozens of cities: Denver, Kansas City, St. Louis, New York, Washington, and always, Chicago.

Buckley's antics were varied and legendary. Using his remarkable physical prowess and training as a lumberjack to good advantage, Dick combined wit with dazzling stunts to keep his audience spellbound.

From the stage he'd heckle the floor judge (who was making sure the dancers fulfilled the requirements of the competition), threatening him with a wet towel and a bucket of water. When the poor, set-upon official could tolerate the abuse no longer, he would chase Dick up into the balcony with furious threats of retribution. Dick, running nimbly just ahead of the judge, escaped his just desserts by 'fleeing' out across the balcony banister – a narrow strip of wood located some thirty feet above the auditorium floor. Balancing on the banister with apparent ease, Buckley would further taunt his pursuer, until, just as he happened to be located in front of the most beautiful girl in the theater immediately below him, he'd 'lose his balance' and tumble innocently into the surprised woman's lap. Once situated in such a desirable locale, Buckley would suavely ignore the lady's escort and make whatever proposal he felt he could finesse. Luckily, he was big and fast, and seldom was he ever seriously threatened by jealous escorts. The audience went wild.

At other times, he would climb to the steel beams supporting the ceiling and strip down to his shorts – throwing his clothes down to fellow emcee Jimmy Bitner. Or 'roll' a large water jug across a banister like he had rolled logs in the lumber camp. Or swing from the rafters on a rope, yelling like Tarzan. One scene that was frequently repeated involved a mock wrestling match between Dick and five or six of his compatriots, in which Buckley's brand-new suit would be ripped from his body during the melee. Sporting fancy flowered shorts, Buckley would then allow his fellow performers to throw him into a blanket and bounce him high into the air.

Responding to the cheers of the audience, Dick would order them to throw him ever higher, until his weary tormenters could no longer lift their arms. "Dick was impossible to follow," said the Sloniger Brothers, who appeared with him in many of the walkathons of the time. "You never knew what he was going to do. He had more fun than anyone."

By now known as the "Midnight Maniac" and the "California Chatterbox," Buckley could afford such an expensive skit because he was among the highest paid

entertainers in his profession (and too, he had an arrangement with his tailor). So popular had he become, that local
clubs such as the Ball of Fire and the Suzy Q provided him
with constant bookings between his walkathon tours.

Rudi Valle saw Buckley in '33: "I loved him because he
was a crazy bastard; he always had a cigarette and a drink in
his hand." To warm the crowds up, he'd fake putting his
finger up his nose and then put his finger in his drink to stir
before drinking it.

In addition to his reputation as a performer, Dick
Buckley was rapidly gaining notoriety for his elegant lifestyle
and wild lascivious parties. Whenever he was seen around
town, his chauffeured limousine and impeccable tuxedo were
the two tell-tale signs people never forgot. Two Great Danes
were often at his side, and a beautiful woman – often blonde
– was surely nearby.

When he would visit his hometown of Stockton in the
huge limo, his overwhelmed family would worry about the
change that had come over their Dick. Feeling confused and
isolated from his world and good fortune, his brothers Jim
and Ben once stole ties out of his suitcase. Dick just shook
his head and laughed, and let them know he didn't care – he
would have given them the ties if they'd asked.

Back in Chicago – his base of operations – Dick lived up to his words. Constantly surrounded by a vast entourage of fans who were hypnotized by his storytelling, and women who were hypnotized by his presence, as well as a host of musicians and other entertainers who reveled in his near-constant partying, Buckley spent, lent, or gave away literally every penny he was making at the time. And in an era when a few cents went a long way, $1500/week went far indeed. His generosity included regular mass migrations to a favorite chicken place where everyone would eat their fill and Dick would sign for it all. His apartment became known as "Mother Buckley's Kitchen" for the constant stream of friends, acquaintances, and hangers-on who literally lived for a few days, weeks, or months off Dick's benevolence.

His 'gang' was a mixed assortment of ages, races, and creeds, bound together by their love of life, their free thinking... and Buckley. He was more than just their host and provider. He was a catalyst for their thoughts, an unequalled source of energy, and most especially, a human being who really cared, loved life and everything it had to offer.

He had experienced abject poverty himself, and knew what it was like to be without paternal guidance and love in a world too big, too cold and hurried to notice. Each and every person he met was important to him, and he felt it to be his responsibility to bring out the best in each of them.

Not that he loved everyone.

Quite the contrary. His patience, especially when he was drinking, could be explosively short. But no one was dismissed off-handedly as too young, or too old, too poor, or too uneducated. The only requirements to be included in the Buckley life scene were a desire to be what you wanted to be, to listen and be entertained, and the ability to accept life without bias or preconception.

Marijuana was smoked regularly at his parties, and cocaine was not unheard of. Sexuality was accepted as a healthy urge and was avidly promoted. The sky was the limit for fun, and Buckley's pad was always open to those hip (wise) enough to enjoy it.

When he was staying in town and not working a walkathon, he appeared at speakeasies not only to bring in extra money, but to broaden his already considerable reputation and give him the opportunity to sharpen his act with new material. During the early 30's, Dick often worked with Ted Swan as his "stooge," and his act ranged from the ridiculous to the obscene.

In one bit, Swan pretended he was fishing as Buckley 'swam' around below him in a fascinating comedy pantomime that probed the sport from the viewpoint of the fish. In another, he described the fate of a French pilot who wrote MERDE in the skies and was shot down in flames. Speaking in a fast, mesmerizing cadence, Dick could master a crowd – especially in a small cafe´ – with overpowering ease, creating the visual impression of the stricken plane so vividly that his exhaled smoke seemed to originate in the burning fuselage.

But oftentimes, as the night wore on and a few drinks found their mark, Buckley could become incredibly acerbic. He didn't often lose his temper, but when a rude or heckling ringsider interrupted Dick Buckley, he had better be ready for the consequences.

His most frequent manner of retaliation began with a dazzling, almost friendly oration directed at the guilty party. With words flowing like a hot shower, Dick would make a point about uncouth behavior so intricately, weaving such a brilliant string of arguments, that his victim would often smile in confused amazement as his head was slipped into the ever-tightening noose.

When Buckley was satisfied he had made his point, he'd bend down toward the heckler, shift his judicial gaze to the poor man's lady escort, and suddenly demand, "Why don't you just take that fucking whore home!?" As the smile vanished from the accused's face, and a brilliant flush filled his lady's cheeks, Buckley joined his audience in a raucous laugh at the retreating couple's expense.

Needless to say, only true masochists and an occasional drunk ever interrupted Dick twice.

A similar tactic was reserved for spectators at the walkathons who couldn't keep their cool while joining Buckley for a short stint onstage. One such fellow, a bit intoxicated and all too belligerent, had his legs handcuffed together to keep him under control. When his verbal abuse became too great for Dick, however, Buckley pushed him off the stage, still handcuffed, with the admonition: "You didn't know anybody here until I put you in the limelight... so now, you SOB, stay down there!"

As more and more people heard of Buckley's extravagant showbiz magic, his salary and prestige in Chicago skyrocketed. It wasn't long before top mob leaders took an interest in the brash yet sophisticated young performer, and soon he numbered them among his many friends and supporters. One such gangster acquaintance, with more money than he could legitimately justify, bought a bankrupt circus on the spur of the moment and invited Dick out to the storage area to inspect his purchase and decide what to do with it.

Never one to miss out on an adventure, no matter how mundane, Buckley hopped into his limo and drove out to inspect the tremendous treasure his friend had acquired. Like a little boy turned loose in his father's old trunk, Dick was enthralled by the multitude of costumes and finery and proceeded to try on anything that looked interesting.

One full-length lavender robe, complete with an impressive array of jewels, captured his eye almost immediately and demanded a proper display before the small assemblage of friends. Parading around with the robe wrapped around his shoulders, his head held high, Dick cut a figure more dashing than comical. But in a moment of gentle ribbing, a buddy captured the image he projected with unwitting precision: "Well, well. If Lord Buckley hasn't arrived."

And so he had.

CHAPTER 3

His Lordship was still Dick Buckley on stage, but increasingly his elegant style and extravagant appearance cemented his lordly title among his friends. Among his legions of fans, however, whatever the name the result was the same: unqualified adulation.

His popularity became so great by 1932 that he became a kingly pawn in the intense competition between two rival walkathon promoters. With he and Red Skelton the only two sure-fire draws, both the Northside and Southside organizations were desperate to obtain his services. When word leaked that Dick was considering making a switch from north to south, his employer sent a couple of his more *persuasive* employees - complete with brass knuckles - to urge Buckley to reconsider.

Fortunately for Dick, however, he was tipped to their visit and made other plans immediately. He drove non-stop to Miami and stayed for nearly a year, playing clubs, working on material, and having a good time. One of his delights was driving, and a spin down by the ocean was a regular time of relaxation. After one particularly successful party, however, he decided that driving near the ocean wasn't half as fun as driving *in* the ocean, and he proceeded to cruise for two miles with the surf lapping at his tires. When he returned to Chicago in 1933, a high-water mark of salt corrosion remained etched in the side of his huge auto.

His first appearance upon returning was a somewhat uncertain experience for Dick, since his prolonged absence had removed him from the mainstream of showbiz and the crowd's reaction was unsure. But when he strode into the Coliseum and saw thousands of standing, screaming fans, even his most optimistic expectations were exceeded. Buckley was back, and they loved it.

Returning to work at the Ball of Fire between walkathons, Dick experimented with a wide variety of acts, not all of which seemed befitting to "that famed British comedian appearing by the grace of the Great Kingdom." For instance, he would climb a ladder onstage while presenting a monologue, unzip his zipper, and pretend to urinate on the floor by pouring a beer he had secreted in his tux. Called the 'piss from the perch,' it was less than elegant but was received with cheers by his enthralled audiences.

Of course, such light-hearted nonsense was a godsend to people praying for an end to the Depression. So too was

Franklin Delano Roosevelt, who assumed the Presidency in January of '33. Life was still miserable for millions of Americans, but hope was born anew and the nation began a long, slow move toward recovery.

In just a few months, Prohibition was repealed, and gangsters and speakeasies began to give way to businessmen and legitimate clubs. The people were often the same, but appearances changed.

On the streets of Chicago, Dick Buckley began to dress, if possible, even more extravagantly. It wasn't at all unusual to see him strolling along, a beautiful lady by his side, dressed in tux and tails, a monocle in his eye and ivory cigarette holder in his hand, but without shoes or socks. Convention be damned! Buckley was interested in generating excitement, awakening interest, not abiding by stuffy conventions and unnecessary rules. So when he married again later in the year, it isn't surprising his bride was Peaches Brownie, the #1 burlesque queen in all of Chicago.

Together they set up housekeeping in a suite near the Royden Hotel, a huge apartment that could – and did – accommodate up to fifty people. There the infamous Three-Year Party began, with continuous revelry at almost all hours of the day and night from 1934 to 1937.

The central room of the apartment was a huge loft area, in which the main body of the congregation hung out – with spillovers hanging *way* out in the bedrooms, bathroom, kitchen, and fire escape.

Blonde bombshells and hookers discussed their separate realities with socialites and writers; the best black jazz musicians in town passed the time with actors, dancers, and pimps. *'Buckley People'* seemed to come from the ends of the spectrum: either extremely independent and self-assured, or totally dependent on His Lordship for everything from food to philosophy. They all wanted some of the fun, the excitement, the thrill of living at the edge of tomorrow. Some came for the sex, some the drugs, but all came for the electricity of life he generated.

In the bustling kitchen, Peaches or Lord Jocko – Buckley's friend and aide – or, later, wife #3 Angel Rice, supervised a big communal pot of mulligan stew. An assortment of alcoholic beverages (by now legal once more) guaranteed that most everyone sipped the drink of their choice. Fat, misshapen cigarettes passed from hand to hand, a wet towel stuffed under the door to keep the sweet smoke within bounds.

During the early hours of the daily get-together, commotion and stimulating conversation were expected and

allowed. As the evening hours passed, however, Dick 'Lord'
Buckley moved to his favorite spot, usually a high-backed
chair, and began to tell stories, recite bits, impersonate
celebrities, joke, and generally involve his guests so
thoroughly that within minutes every eye was turned his way.

First time guests were stunned by the diversity and
intensity of his personality. Buckley the entertainer came to
life whenever he was in a group of more than two... and one
was a stranger. His speech would veer and swerve
unannounced, moving from a polished British
pronouncement to a hip black rap in the lowering of an
eyebrow. And not only did the accent change, but so did the
character. Facial expression, body carriage, hand movements
– they all were transformed magically, and a new Buckley
creation led the gathering off into other worlds without so
much as an announcement of the impending journey.

Conversation among the group continued, but Buckley
dominated the gathering with "completely original material
beyond category." Dick was a master deipnosophist – a
conversationalist so entertaining and exceptional that most
guests never even attempted to interrupt when he was rolling.

Of course, there were times, especially very late at
night after he had drained his glass four or five times too
many, that his sarcasm became painfully pointed and even

domineering. But even such negative moments didn't seem to dampen spirits too long, and many of the same people were regulars at nearly every night's party.

Buckley's practical jokes, a favorite hobby since his childhood, were also received in many ways. At one particularly swinging affair, Dick oversaw the action until discarded clothes nearly buried the empty booze bottles in a spare room, and then excused himself "to get more ice." While the party roared on in his absence, Dick went downstairs and found not only the ice but two friendly uniformed patrolmen with whom he struck up a conversation. As they talked, Buckley became convinced that the two were *'cool'* and invited them up to the party. But, always alert to an ad-lib situation, he asked them if they'd mind waiting just a few moments before coming up. Sneaking upstairs into the room where the clothes were tossed, he tied all the pant legs and sleeves of every garment into knots for his own special surprise.

Rejoining the party, Buckley neglected to mention the meeting to his friends, and reacted casually when a knock sounded on his door. The partyers were too involved in their merriment to pay much attention, but when the door swung open and Buckley's powerful voice bellowed in mock surprise, "Well good evening, *officers!*" the chaos was immediate.

A covey of naked bodies darted for the spare room in panic flight, and their horror mounted when they tried to jump quickly into their clothes. The sound of tearing fabric could be heard above the vehement mutterings of despair, but both were nearly drowned by the roar of Buckley's laughter. When the sound of that laughter finally penetrated the crowded room, Dick immediately transformed a ticklish situation into a good hearty laugh for nearly everyone and introduced the policemen to the reconciled crowd.

Though Chicago had become his home and preferred center of operations, Lord Buckley (as Jocko, David Hecht, called him) continued to tour the nation with Leo Seltzer's walkathons, and increasingly to play theaters and nightclubs as the featured performer.

Sophia LeNart was a young contestant at the 1934 Washington D.C. Walkathon, and she still remembers Dick Buckley 45 years later. "I recall that he arrived in a Rolls Royce with his chauffeur-valet. Dick was dressed in tails and top-hat; he made quite an elegant entrance to say the least. We contestants always looked forward to having him as emcee - he added *class* to the show."

"I remember him singing *"In Your Easter Bonnet,"* the song for which he had the most requests. He also had a request practically every night to do his special *'The Face On the Barroom Floor.'"*

The day Dick was leaving D.C. after that performance, an old friend, Mike Gould, stopped by to visit and catch up on recent events. Mike found Buckley in the company of a beautiful 19-year-old socialite, whose parents were among the most wealthy and influential families of the Capital.

At dinner that night, the reminiscing and laughter continued, with the doting young woman hanging on Dick's every word. When it finally came time for them to part, and Dick to catch a train, Mike was the recipient of an unexpected gift.

"This is for you, Lord Michael," he said with a mischievous grin as he indicated his escort. "My compliments."

Though laughter covered the shock and surprise, neither Mike nor the young lady ever learned if Dick was joking or serious in his offer, though the latter is probably more likely.

Traveling north to New York, Dick played the Palace Theater with three bits that became his trademark for the remainder of the decade and beyond. The best-known and

longest-lasting routine was called the Four Person
Pantomime, in which Dick practiced his self-developed *mass
pantomimicism*. "I went through the various scenes and
movements of showbusiness, and finally I achieved the thing
called Mass Pantomimicism, which is the art of voice
projection through people. It's employed and controlled by a
thing called Sticata Control, which is a system of piercing
touch, a lightning touch, preceded by a very strong sound,
which when you project these voices magnificent things
happen."

Beginning with four *volunteers* (three men and a woman
– originally from the band, but later from the audience),
Buckley *commanded* his subjects to come up on stage and take
their places in chairs arranged in a straight line, side-by-side.
Usually, Dick's presence and powerful voice alone were
sufficient to persuade even the most reticent participant to
take part, but when faced with a truly unwilling party he
resorted first to cajolery and then sarcasm to motivate them.
It was rare indeed for a person to ignore a full-fledged
Buckley effort, so intense was the energy he radiated.

"It is very simple," he said, "I look at you, I pick you,
and you come with me. The day I can't do that, I'm finished."

Once onstage, Dick assigned each participant a seat
and then chatted with them for just a moment to relax them.

Then, scatting a few bars of "*Sunny Side of The Street,*" he presented each with a unique hat to delineate the character they were to represent.

"Ladies and gentlemen," he intoned as he took a seat behind but within easy reach of all four subjects, "a study in mass pantomimicism. To the lovely lady and the three gentlemen seated upon the chairs: through these four charming people I will project four different and distinct voices. Each and every one of them will be given an individual voice to pantomime. They themselves will not say word one. When they hear the voice assigned to them come through the microphone, they will move their lips, eyebrows, nose, facial contours, and whatnot in a PANTOMIMIC manner, thereby simulating actual speech." As he spoke, in a lightning-fast British accent, he touched his four subjects to establish his presence and adjusted their seats to facilitate his task.

Moving from left to right (as the audience viewed it), he introduced the characters to be portrayed in his little drama. "Now this handsome rascal here will have the voice of Andy. That's a very deep voice: 'Ahh, it look like everything gonna be fine and dandy,'" came the distinctive bass voice, and the gentleman moved his lips as though speaking while Lord Buckley tapped him on the back.

"You lad," he continued, "will have the voice of Brother Crawfish: 'Well my dear boy, I dare say I don't think of the matter one way or the other.' Her Highness the Queen will have the voice of Madame Queen, a very high sort: 'I tol' you boys!' And His Lordship here will have the voice of Amos: 'Well Judge, you gotta change your talk or you ain't never comin' back!'

"Now we are going to play LITTLE THEATER!" The band played a flourish. "Ladies and gentlemen, you are about to witness the first mass pantomime broadcast of Amos and Andy. The time is... the *summertime*, the warm golden summertime of Southern California.

"They're seated in a LOVELY Spanish garden, in the fabulous San Fernando Valley, and it's SUNDOWN, and the MOON, that beautiful Southern California moonlight, is shining right down in their eyes. They're looking up into the moonlight, they've got a double shot of tequila apiece, and a very NEW California drink called a Benzedrine Float. Andrew is speaking."

Lord Buckley put the four volunteers to the test with an intricate, fast-paced performance that began with a short segment related to current events (or personal idiosyncrasies if the subject was a celebrity) and moved through a hilarious physicalization of a heavy drinker awakening with a terrible hangover (a subject His Lordship knew all-too-well), finishing ten minutes later with a romantic interlude between Amos and Madame Queen.

Not only was the black dialect accurate, but the illusion he created was so real that many of his subjects became involved to the extent they totally forgot they were on stage. Their initial shock, even embarrassment, at speaking like a black person, gave way to acceptance and – occasionally – even a glint of greater understanding. The affair between Amos and Madame Queen that climaxed the bit occasionally generated such torrid love-making that Buckley was forced to break the clinch to avoid embarrassing consequences (and police raids!)

At the conclusion of the Pantomime, Dick would often demonstrate his version of an old Vaudeville favorite: the hat-switch routine.

A simple piece of business, the entire bit consisted of nothing more than Dick and one of his volunteers standing facing each other, switching hats between them to the rhythm provided by the band. But Buckley's magic transformed even so basic an act into a supremely funny sequence. By feigning, hesitating, and generally confusing his partner, Dick kept his audience laughing from beginning to end.

Of greater significance than either of his two biggest laugh-getters, however, was a short skit that presaged the hip material Buckley introduced publicly in the late 40's. While most comedians of the era were classic stand-up types whose stock in trade were the one-liners and rehashed punch-line stories, Buckley foresaw the more involved, evocative humor of the 60's and 70's and began refining such artistic comedy in the mid-Thirties.

On a darkened stage, with a single spot following his every move, Dick danced a graceful waltz... with a hatbox as his partner. With an insane glimmer in his eyes, he finished the dance and then began to talk to the hatbox, his voice low and bedeviled. Twisting his moustache in demonic delight, he reached into the box and pulled out a woman's head, a gory masterpiece of wax that always brought gasps from the unsuspecting audience and giggles from the band.

Holding the head at arm's length, he stared into its eyes and intoned solemnly, "You made one mistake my dear... You slammed the door!"

By 1934, Buckley had developed a strong nationwide following, having appeared in nearly every city of size from coast to coast. But of all the many places he played, three stood out: New York – the "Big Apple", the city in which he was forced to eat from trash cans on that first try at the bigtime; Hollywood, with its big stars and big dreams; and, of course, Chicago, the one city that really understood and accepted him as a superstar.

Returning to Chicago after his eastern tour, Dick played the Arcadia Gardens arena, a giant auditorium five stories tall. Red Skelton and he were co-headliners, and thousands of fans paid their 25-cent admission to see the best of the walkathon emcees in head-to-head competition. And that's just what it amounted to at times. Buckley was usually the late man, coming on at midnight and playing til the wee hours with Skelton immediately preceding him. Their rivalry was generally friendly, but on at least one occasion Buckley's practical jokes strained the relationship. Red was widely-known for a drunk act, complete with pratfalls, that centered on a prop gin bottle. Skelton made clever use of props in his act, lots of them, and he was dead without them. One night, Dick arrived early and hid the bottle, pretending to have no knowledge of its whereabouts while Red searched frantically. When Skelton found out that Dick was responsible for its disappearance, a chill fell over their relationship that was to last, at least in part, until Red made his move into films.

As might be expected with Dick's notoriety and the late hours he performed, his audience was always liberally dotted with Chicago's *night people*. In 1934, one of those was a

13-year-old newsboy by the name of Cy Green, who would hawk the early edition of the local paper to the huge captive crowd. Cy remembers his first meeting with Buckley "as though it were yesterday."

"Dick was up on stage doing his act when I happened to walk in front of the stage selling my papers.

"'Ladies and gentlemen,' Buckley suddenly announces, 'here is a poor street urchin selling his papers at 1:30 in the morning when he should be home sleeping for school.'

"He has me come up on stage and tells everyone 'he's selling papers to support his widowed mother. Let's help this little guttersnipe out. He should be home in bed, asleep.' He really laid on the sympathy bit, and sure as hell, here comes a gigantic shower of change thrown from the audience onto the wooden floor. While the band played, a janitor came out and swept up all the money and gave it to me. As I remember, it was something like $280!"

Backstage, Cy thanked Buckley with wide eyes; the immaculately-dressed emcee responded by talking with the youngster for a half hour and turning him on to his first marijuana high. "For three years," Cy recalls, "whenever the walkathon came back, we'd pull the same scam and always pick up more money that I'd normally see in a year."

As their friendship grew, Dick helped the youngster in other ways as well. One afternoon, Buckley explained to his young charge that they were going to visit a very wealthy home and meet a very lovely lady. "Don't get dressed up though," Dick explained, "look terrible, because today she is going to do us both a favor." A large chauffeured limo picked them up and drove them out to Wilmette, where they met Paulette, a French madam friend of Buckley's. "This is my illegitimate son, and we've got to get him some clothes," Dick said by way of introduction. She took him to Marshall Fields, one of the finest stores in Chicago, and bought him a complete new wardrobe. He looked so good, all his "guttersnipe" friends were envious.

A short time later, Dick played a walkathon on the westside at the Golden-Pumpkin Room. His arrival was widely heralded, and the room was packed his opening night. The next night, however, without explanation he didn't appear. It was a week later that his fans learned that Dick had been kidnapped and held until he agreed to leave the show on the westside and emcee the Southside show at the Coliseum.

With such insane pressures constantly surrounding him, it's not surprising Dick began to drink more heavily, or that his drinking got him into some difficult moments. Never one to shirk a fight, and even less likely to do so when bombed, on several occasions he sought-out battles for the excitement they generated. Totally sloshed at a local bar one night, he walked outside and accosted passersby with a variety of harangues. One particularly mean-looking fellow was walking his attractive lady down the street when Dick greeted them with all his charm and aplomb.

"You, my dear, are a princess," he intoned graciously to the woman, "and you sir," he directed toward her dubious escort, "you are a shit!"

Unfortunately, where many such confrontations by Buckley would dissolve into a heated exchange of sarcasm, this particular gentleman was in no mood to match wits with Dick. Instead, he levelled him with a quick, unannounced barrage of fists. By the time worried friends helped Dick to his feet, the couple was gone, and so, shrugging at his misfortune, he verbally lambasted the man in absentia for his poor attitude, praised him for his punch, and went back into the bar to quaff a few more tall ones.

Such escapades got Dick into more than his share of disagreements, yet because of his size and the glibness of his tongue, few ever went the distance to punches. Whether inside a theater or out, Buckley's remarkable mind was never at a loss for a quick-repartee, a subtle slam, or even a face-saving explanation if the situation required. Admiration, esteem, and wonderment were mixed with vexation when Dick was in his cups, however, and even his close friends and wives were not immune to the verbal, and occasional physical abuse he could unleash in a drunken rage. Such anger was infrequent, thankfully, and Buckley lost few friends or admirers because of it.

In fact, Buckley made new friends and won new admirers virtually every day of his life, at times transforming lives with the intensity of his beliefs and the honesty of his lifestyle. Bret Howard met Buckley at a Denver walkathon in the Thirties, and her life was never the same:

"When I met Dick Buckley, I was twelve years of age and dressed-up to look like I was sixteen. I was going to a girls' finishing school, and I had a very great friend who played the drums and was sort of a revolutionary. He felt that I was very bright and I could dance and do all sorts of things; I had all these plans to complete finishing school.

"Well, I was allowed to have a night out – my family gave him visiting privileges, and so he could take me out. He was 16 or 17 and he was interested in radio, and his friend was the manager of a radio station which was broadcasting the Walkathon. So we had tickets to the show, but I was underage.

"At the time, I had long hair halfway down my back, and I was five-foot-ten, but still they took all of my hair and piled it on top of my head. Then they put high heels on me and dressed me up. By the time they got through with me, I can't imagine what I must have looked like.

"And so we went to this huge auditorium where they had the Walkathon. I can't explain it to you, but anyway, I had never been in a place like that. It was a circus-night like, and they had whiskey on the side, real raw stuff. But I was very sophisticated for a twelve-year-old girl, in an intellectual sense of the word. I had gone to Europe and everything. So that's why my friends had figured that I could carry it off.

"We had box seats and everything, and the radio station manager, who sat with us, was very friendly with this Buckley. Anyway, they never figured that we would be invited to come to his dressing room. But we were, and we went in.

"I'll never forget that scene as long as I live. I had never known another human being that had had the magnetism that he had. There was a black cat there, and there was this little hooker who had been working in the Walkathon, and she didn't even have enough money to make her way out. He was just handing out what looked like thousands of dollars, and there were people coming in, saying that they wouldn't be able to make it another night. It was really wild. I'm sure it was his whole week's salary.

"I was sitting on the sofa, and he got out some bootleg whiskey and started directing this whole act towards me. I wasn't aware of it at the time, but I'm sure he felt there was some kind of kindred spirit there. But there was no way he could have guessed that I was the age I was – I must have looked at least 18 or something.

"I had just had my first drink of whiskey in my life, with nothing to wash it down with except Coca Cola, and he gets up and starts telling this magnificent story. And you talk about a shocker of bringing a girl into the reality of showbusiness! He told a story about a place where he had been working, I don't know where it was but it must have been another walkathon, and he had gotten 'the clap' and he began playing his ukulele and saying 'I was singing away, singing away,' and I didn't know what the hell he was talking about.

"He was so magnificently good-looking – I can tell you, in my life I've met many people with sexual magnetism, but I've never known another human being that had it like his. And the funniest part about his sexual magnetism was that he was always surrounded with groups. He was never alone – he always had this on-drive.

"Anyway, the song that he closed the walkathon with that evening was *"Good Night Sweetheart,"* and when I went back to finishing school and turned on the radio, I would hear Dick Buckley singing *"Good Night Sweetheart"* and was convinced he was singing it to me. It had to be – I was sure he wouldn't sing it to anyone else in the world!"

With such overwhelming personal attraction, it was only a matter of time before someone realized Buckley deserved a place of his own. And so, in 1936, racketeers financed *Chez Buckley*, a small tavern located in Chicago at the SE corner of Roscoe and Western.

As the attraction extraordinaire of the club, Dick was promised 25% of the take in addition to a hefty salary. The club was intimate, with just a few tables, a small dance floor, a service bar and bandstand, but the place was always jumping with the hotshots of the underworld set. Buckley's wit and general pluck ingratiated him with his clientele, and Al Capone himself was an acknowledged fan.

In his own club, with an audience who appreciated his talents and understood at least most of his performance, Dick was free to turn loose and give them more than they counted on. To back him in his efforts, he recruited the best jazz musicians in town – most of whom were black. Dick wasn't colorblind, he just wanted the best players and the freest thinkers.

Aside from his usual routines, Dick improvised some of his zaniest moments onstage at Chez Buckley, secure in his role as a favorite of the big-guys. Always arriving well-warmed for the show, Dick walked briskly through the audience to the table nearest the stage, placed a glass of beer on top of a chair, stacked the chair on top of the table, and then with no approach whatsoever leapt over the entire structure and landed upright onstage to begin his show. Though there were only two ceiling fans in the entire club to dissipate the stifling Chicago summer heat, Buckley ordered them shut off when he was performing; they were distracting.

His act was similar to his *Ball of Fire* appearances, though even more spontaneous and ad-libbed. Drawing long and hard on a bulging cigarette, and holding the smoke interminably, he called upon his audience to supply a watch for a trick he wanted to demonstrate. When he found a cooperative victim, he took just a few seconds to place the watch on the floor with a flourish, instruct everyone to keep their eyes on it, and then crush it into the floorboards with his shoe. Off-handed apologies brought laughs from the audience when the mangled timepiece was revealed, and only fast talking saved Dick from a beating.

On another occasion, not even his fast wits could have saved him. Ranging through the audience as he described a magnificent feat he was about to perform, Dick graciously borrowed every fur coat he could find – and despite the heat, the beautiful molls had quite a collection. Returning to the stage, he ceremoniously made a large pile in the middle of the floor and, continuing a fast-paced monologue about the wondrous demonstration, he nonchalantly proceeded to squirt lighter fluid over the coats and casually set them on fire! Even as his monologue continued, the shock and disbelief of his audience quickly turned to anger as a crew came out to extinguish the blaze. Several unsavory characters were motivated to head toward the stage, and Buckley looked like he was in for a bad time of it until a loud guffaw sounded from the very back of the club. There sat one of the head honchos of Chicago's gangland society, and he thought the whole incident was hilarious.

"Thank you, Your Grace," Buckley intoned with a sign of relief, "it's good to see *someone* possesses a sense of humor in the midst of this deplorable situation."

His attackers stopped dead in their tracks. Some managed a weak chuckle; others forced a grin through clenched teeth. But it wasn't until the Boss offered to replace all the coats that the tension eased below lynching level.

Perhaps that animosity remained just under the surface. Perhaps the incident was never forgotten. In any case, a few weeks later Buckley's luck ran out. He was more than a little inebriated from an assortment of intoxicants, and was in the midst of a rambling monologue when a mobster sitting right up front decided it was time for Dick to get on with the more mundane elements of his show. A bit looped himself, the thug got a touch mouthy and loud with his insulting opinions, and it wasn't long at all before Dick had had enough.

It wasn't bad enough he should question the hood's heritage, parentage, and masculinity. Oh no, Dick Buckley wasn't about to stop there once he got rolling. When he felt he had sufficiently destroyed his heckler, he turned his attention on the man's escort.

No woman alive could've possessed the attributes and accomplished the physical feats Dick attributed to her. And no self-respecting gangster in Chicago could've let the matter slide.

When Dick stepped off-stage briefly to take a breather a half-hour later, he was met in the wings by two of the hood's associates, who took Buckley out into the alley and expressed their boss's extreme displeasure with Dick's performance.

A trifle late on his musical cue to return, Dick dragged himself onstage spitting blood and pulling loose teeth from his mouth. There was no doubt what had happened, and yet no question in his mind that he was going on.

"Very good," he whispered into the microphone, "but what do you do for an encore?"

For an instant the crowd was silent. Then with an outlaw's respect for bravado and sheer guts, they exploded in an ovation that even included his adversary. Dick continued with the show, and his reputation emerged not only intact but aggrandized.

Such feats as wiring a car parked behind the club for sound and then hiring two hookers to take unsuspecting patrons out there for a brief episode of *'Candid Car Seat'* brought a steady throng to the club. Unfortunately, the 25% cut he was supposed to receive never materialized, and he left *Chez Buckley* after only three weeks.

All the while The Party continued, however, though the location had moved to 1205 N. State St., on the second floor. After one show, he invited Joe Danno and the *'Cats & Fiddle'* music group to stop by, and they all travelled to the apartment together in Buckley's huge Cadillac. After they'd parked, they were walking down the street just a few yards from his doorway, when Dick suddenly grabbed the elbow of

a complete stranger who was walking by and swept him
upstairs.

His startled and confused protestations were drowned
out by Buckley's reassurances, and he finally surrendered to
his fate. Ushering them all inside, Dick instructed everyone to
take a seat and relax, which everyone did – as best they could.
Without warning or explanation, Dick began to take off all
his clothes, until he stood before the group stark naked.

The stranger's wide eyes grew even larger when Dick
clapped his hands and ordered someone in the next room to
enter. Into the party came Peaches, in all her naked splendor,
pretending to be hypnotized and under Buckley's complete
control. He ordered her to greet his guests, and she
proceeded to kiss all of them – including the delirious
stranger – on the mouth.

Some marijuana was passed around, and some booze
consumed, and before too long the dazed newcomer was
singing along with the *Cats & Fiddle* and enjoying himself as
he had probably never done before. It was hours later he
remembered his wife was expecting him, and with some
trepidation left the gathering and went home to explain his
absence to the little woman.

Of course, The Party continued, and similar
occurrences took place almost daily. A few weeks later, Dick

decided to give an art class, and directed his aide at the time, Jack Sydell, to go out and bring back all the crates he could find. After a short while, Jack returned with three taxi cabs full of old crates, and the group brought them up to the apartment where Dick smashed them into kindling.

Despite the summer heat, Buckley built a roaring fire. Then he directed Peaches to take off her clothes and lie down on a white bear skin rug, where each guest was given the opportunity to pose her so the class could paint her portrait by the flickering lights of the fire. Not surprisingly, the class was a great success.

During these impromptu get-togethers, Dick not only partied with his friends but entertained them with his old standards as well as new pieces of material so radical that some in the audience were unable to understand them. Dick began developing his hip monologues, and even toyed with the idea of a religious hip translation of the life of Christ in the vein of '*The Nazz.*' Constant refinement served not only to help Dick flesh-out his new material, but also educated his friends to the bits and gave them a rare glimpse of a world yet to be born.

As a favorite son of the metropolis, Buckley was recognized wherever he went in the Windy City. Of course, his dashing good looks, massive limousine, two Great Danes, beautiful wife, and racoon coat might have drawn attention even without his reputation as the hippest, most original and captivating entertainment personality in town.

Most likely the majority of city-folk who saw him ride by had no idea he was usually stark naked under the heavy coat he wore, but if they did it only added to the legend. As did his promotion for a 1937 club gig at the *Ball of Fire*.

With the walkathons feeling pressure from legit theaters and the changing times, Dick was anxious to increase his stature as a club performer by attracting as many of his old fans as possible to his new locale. The entertainment competition in Chicago was intense, and in addition to Milton Berle, Red Skelton, and many others who came out of the walkathons, Dick was matched against Danny Thomas, who played at the 5100 Club just down the street.

Newspaper ads were still the most accepted means of advertising a club date at that time, although radio was coming on strong. But Dick didn't intend to rely on either media, preferring something a bit more personal to announce his upcoming appearance at the *Ball*. So he hired a large flatbed truck, scammed an ornate casket, and persuaded Cy Green to drive him around town decked out in his tux, lying full-length in the casket. Signs on either side of the truck informed inquisitive bystanders *"The Body Will Come To Life*

At The Ball of Fire," with the date, hour and address. Buckley remained perfectly still in his restrictive case for most of the long journey throughout the city, sitting up only when a familiar burning scent would prompt him to order Cy, "Don't smoke all the shit!"

Occasional tours still took Buckley to all parts of the country (e.g. Philadelphia, where he once feigned telephoning J. Edgar Hoover from his hotel room to frighten the local police into dropping some inconsequential charges, and actually called his friends the Jones Brothers), but he always returned to his adopted home town.

There he made *Planet Mars* and the *Ball of Fire* into *the* chic clubs in town for upwardly mobile Northsiders, who were considerably more plentiful as the Depression slowly lessened. The clubs became "a more free and natural *Playboy After Dark*," as did his apartment on Rush Street. A new woman, Angel Rice, came into his life, and the two of them made quite a striking pair: he tall, handsome with dark hair, and she 5'4", blonde and beautiful.

Angel had sung professionally, and Buckley used her in his club dates as an unannounced visitor from the audience. At other times they would recreate the Svengali routine they had developed in their apartment with friends, with Angel as the subject and Dick the infamous hypnotist.

The *Singapore Restaurant* was a favorite celebrity hangout of the day, and Buckley would frequently recruit guests for parties at his "mad pad" from there. Al 'Junior' Lyons would cook a huge roast for the multitude, who would dive into the meal with all the fervor and finesse of Henry VIII – tearing off chunks of meat with their bare hands and throwing bones and refuse over their shoulders.

As the sole provider for such magnificent orgies of delight, Buckley spent a prodigious amount of money: all he earned, plus a little more. If he wanted something, he got it. If he wanted to do something, he did it. If a friend needed a hand, he extended it. As Carl Hoff recalls, "He was a paradox – he could be so brash and bizarre, and then turn right around and be sensitive and sympathetic with people."

One young lady who met Buckley in 1937 understood both sides of his personality, but was drawn to the dashing, magnetic entertainer as if "it had to be." Just a teenager, Lady Paula Kaleel had fled an unhappy marriage to "go out and see what life was all about.

"I went into this particular club in Chicago – it was the *Planet Mars*, and right under the "L" – there he was. He was diggin' me sitting there; we were both pretty young, and I had never seen anything like him in my life.

"He said, 'Wait for me after the show,' so I waited through three performances... in my new knit orange suit. God. It was meant to be that way."

Nine months later, on Dec. 8, 1937, Lady Paula gave birth to a son, Fredrick – and Buckley was an unknowing father. Fifteen months later, Lady Paula heard he was in town and decided "I've got to go see this man and inform him.

"I didn't want anything from him; he was pretty frantic at the time. And, though I was a very young girl, I would not have really chosen him as a father at that time. He seemed a little far-out. I guess I had a lot of strange ideas.

"When I told him, he said, 'Isn't that wonderful!' and patted Fred on the head. He had his entourage with him, and he seemed very pleased by it all."

Lady Paula, like many of those who knew Buckley, was a strong individualist outside of Dick's sphere of influence. "I was really digging it, having the kid all by myself," she explains.

And luckily so, for it would be years before Buckley and Lady Paula would meet again, and more than a decade before Fred would learn his father's identity. For Dick was a changeling, capable of extreme love and generosity at the same time he showed "a mean streak that could scare ya!" The same held true for his professional life onstage.

If an audience didn't respond as well as expected, he'd attack the whole room. "You people are all just a bunch of goddam squares! Who needs you?" And yet at the very next show he might help out a needy kid, as he did with Cy Green and, in 1938, Bob Baxter.

Baxter was just sixteen years old, busking in the Loop for spare change, when he wandered into a club Buckley was playing. Bob asked the club owner if he could pass the hat, and was told to talk to Buckley, who invited him onstage. Dick appreciated that the hat Bob carried was for more than keeping his head dry, and immediately put $1 in the derby and passed it into the audience with his fervent suggestion that everyone should contribute.

"I have here a travelling mountebank, ladies and gentlemen. Let us show our charity and contribute to his education." After collecting a tidy sum, he called Bobby over to join him – at a table with three woman fans. As he chatted with them, Dick nonchalantly slipped his hand up one of the girl's dresses and continued his conversation as he perused her thigh. Then he took Bobby's hand and slid it as far up her leg as it could go, with the instructions, "Feel that flesh, man! It's firm, solid meat!" All the while he mollified the girl with a constant stream of compliments. "You are a beautiful lass, my dear. Marvelously constructed."

Such outrageous antics won Baxter's devotion immediately, as did Dick's stage presence. "At that time, nobody ever swore onstage, not even *damn*," Bobby recalls, "But Buckley didn't care, he'd say whatever he felt. You should have seen the faces when he'd say *fuck* up there. They were terrified!"

With a flair straight out of a Barrymore picture (he was Dick's idol and occasional drinking buddy), Buckley would conclude his show by draining a drink and throwing the empty glass over his shoulder to smash offstage. One night, the entire audience got into the act by emulating their leader, and dozens of glasses smashed against walls all over the club.

But Dick was such a successful draw the club owner needed more than just such minor irritations to ask him to leave. The Mayor of Chicago saw it otherwise, however. As longtime friend George Von Physter tells it:

"Buckley was doing his four-person hat act, and this particular evening the Mayor was in the audience. Buckley invited him up to take a chair, but the Mayor refused; Buckley invited him again and the Mayor refused again. Well, Buckley – no man to be refused – blew his top and began a tirade at the politician from the stage, calling him every conceivable name he could think of, until finally he decided to give up on it and went ahead and did his act.

"Well, they let him finish the act and that was about the size of it. For, when the act was over, a couple of boys came up and grabbed Buckley and told him that if the sun set on him one more day in Chicago, they had a bucket of tar and a bale of feathers they were going to roll him up in. After this run-in, of course, Buckley left town for a while."

During this brief exile, Dick appeared in Portland, Oregon as a radio announcer, and was hired by a wealthy businessman to attend his parties and insult people. Dick would show up in his tuxedo, and with his regal bearing and ramrod posture would instantly create the impression that he was some visiting diplomat or foreign dignitary. Of course, neither His Lordship nor his host bothered to clarify the misconception, and so it was something of a shock when this dignified personality suddenly began to turn on his fellow guests with a subtle, yet unmistakable rapier wit that cut a broad swathe through the crowd.

After just a few weeks, Dick returned to Chicago and picked up where he had left off, though playing more at the *Suzy Q* and *Planet Mars* than the *Ball of Fire*. During one gig at the *Suzy Q*, Dick closed his show with *"The Prisoner Song"* and announced to the audience that the police were there to arrest him. Sure enough, he was charged with rape and picked up as soon as he left the stage. But he somehow convinced his jailers to release him nightly so he could continue his appearance at the club, and so for several nights he showed up at the *Suzy Q* with a police escort. Within a week the charges were completely withdrawn.

During the summer of '38 Dick worked in a resort town fifty miles from Chicago with a six- member group that included Art Sanders, Harry Kiesler, Jim Pendergast, and Fred Reczuch (then Richards), who described the scene:

"During that summer's engagement at this resort in Fox Lake, IL, the nightclub/pavilion was named *"Three Star Hennessey."* It consisted of a main building over the lake and several cottages close by (rentals for summer guests.) Included in the complex was a big two-story house. The girls of the floor show (approx. 6) slept on the first floor, and all the musicians – including the emcee/comic, Dick Buckley, slept on the second floor. So you can understand we lived as one family and frankly, had a ball all summer.

"In that period, Dick had a partner by the name of Al Lyons – who was billed as the stooge. Although Dick always referred to him (publicly) as Junior. Also, we had guest artists, including Anita O'Day and others.

"To describe Dick as a person is easy: he was a very sensitive and yet outgoing person. He liked the simple things in life, but was a flashy dresser. He preferred English riding habits, and would carry a cane, or riding crop. He cut a very fancy figure, and with his adopted English accent, people couldn't help but take to him. He was a sparkling conversationalist and could shade any conversation into a howling melee. He had a way with words, and I believe that was his secret for success. People came from Chicago and other places just to enjoy his shows. They always left laughing.

"You could never get to dislike Dick, even when he criticized you, because he almost always managed to make you laugh afterwards. During that summer's engagement, Dick was to be the star in the show. When Dick had the floor, there was complete silence – you could tell Dick had the audience eating out of his hands. They would clamor for more, and more.

"I remember Dick telling me once that when he got on the floor, he studied his audience for response laughs and would single out only those who would not laugh at his antics. He said: Once you find out what it takes to make that guy laugh, you'll have the rest of the audience rolling in the aisles. And he was so right. After the floor show, Dick could always be seen as a guest at some table of admirers. He had a unique style in his presentation, and as far as I was concerned, he was all alone in his field. Dick was offered big paying jobs, at top nightclubs, if only he would clean up his act and avoid some of the street language he used in his acts. But Dick was Dick, and preferred to do his thing on his own terms.

"I don't mean to imply that Dick was vulgar or crude. It's just that he used a loose language in his show that most all entertainment people used in private. I believe the audience liked to be shocked. Otherwise, why would they come back, time after time?

"From the very beginning of our relationship, Dick took to me and I in turn took to him. We used to have Mondays as our day off, and when Dick would go into Chicago on business I would tag along. We got along very well – sharing our innermost secrets, ambitions, and dreams. One of his plans for the future was to live in a small town, where everybody knew everybody. On our jaunts to Chicago and back to Fox Lake, he would point out the beauty of the countryside, the pretty farms, the horses, and cattle. He loved the open country.

"On one of our visits in downtown Chicago, we were strolling on a sidewalk and, of course, Dick was dressed to kill in the English riding habit including leather riding boots and of course twirling his cane (or was it the riding crop?) when we approached two portly and very proper society-type ladies.

Their jaws dropped in amazement and they stopped walking, probably wondering who this character was. Dick and I continued to walk past these two gals, and Dick pretended not to notice them, when all of a sudden he whirled around and started to gaze at them in return. They were so surprised by his act, they turned two shades of pink in embarrassment and practically galloped away.

"That was Dick. You could not intimidate or embarrass him – no how. A little more about Dick's personality: When I first met him, I was 25 years of age. Dick never did mention his age, so I had no idea how old he was. Nor did he talk much about his past. I don't recall that Dick had any heroes in or out of showbiz. He would on occasion lampoon the establishment by parodies while onstage. He never, to my knowledge, talked about his future ambition or aspirations. He seemed content to live day to day, enjoying what life had to offer at that time – except, of course, he did have a soft spot to someday live in a small town.

"Dick had the ability to squeeze fun out of each living day, and always seemed to be able to make life for everyone a fun thing. He did this almost like a religion. He must have been inwardly inspired and motivated to feel a compulsion to make people laugh. It was almost as if he felt the good Lord brought him on this earth for specifically just that. He was a comic – on and off the stage. I remember when we (the whole gang) had meals together boarding house style. He would be clearly in charge of the conversation – but always in the lighter vein. I have never seen Dick in a 'blue' mood. Dick was not only gracious, but patient with coworkers. He had an ability to get the most out of them; consequently, people liked and respected him.

"He was not a temperamental tyrant who used people for personal gain. As far as his temper was concerned, he kept it under control. In the three months I worked with Dick, I saw him blow his cork only two times. Let me explain:

"When Dick came to *3 Star Hennessey's* with us, he had a pet monkey named Baby. For the most part Baby would spend most of each day in a portable cage. But Dick would put a leash on this monkey, and there existed a relationship between them, almost like father and son. Well, one day while Dick was attempting to attach the leash to the monkey's collar, the monkey got away and all hell broke loose.

"The first thing the monkey did was to jump to the first tree he could see; the country there was full of trees – like a giant forest. I was standing by when this happened and could see that Dick was quite upset. He could visualize losing the monkey forever.

"The monkey climbed up the tree (way up to the top, about 65-75 feet high) and apparently had a ball with this new freedom – which he undoubtedly had for the first time. Dick started to talk to Baby in nice even tones, but the monkey paid no attention at all. Now Dick knew Baby loved bananas, so he dashed into the house for one; meanwhile, Dick asked me to keep my eyes on the monkey because the trees were so thick and so close together you could hardly see it. In about two minutes, out comes Dick, with a peeled banana in his hand, looking quite worried.

"He walked up to the tree and said: "Here, Baby! Daddy's got a nice fresh banana for you." The monkey paid no attention; in fact, he hopped to an adjacent treetop and gave Dick that independent look and ignored him. Dick continued: 'Baby, please come down to Daddy and have this nice sweet banana.' The monkey jumped to another tree and Dick and I followed.

"Well, 15 or 20 minutes later, the monkey was having a ball and Dick was practically on his knees begging the monk to come down. Finally, Dick blew his cool and in a loud voice yelled, 'Come down you son-of-a-bitch, or I'll climb this damn tree and get you.'

"The next day the monkey finally came down, because he had nothing to eat. Dick had no problem coaxing him into his cage – with a nice, sweet banana.

"The only other time Dick blew his cool, also involved the monkey. You see, Baby loved beer. I suspect Dick got him hooked on beer, probably as a lark. The boys in the band also knew that the monkey loved beer, and that's how the trouble began.

"When Dick would start his show, he would bring Baby along and chain him to a stair railing at the rear of the pavilion (the service entrance), and there the monkey would spend the whole evening climbing and horsing around – as monkeys do. During Dick's break, he would check the monkey on and off. When the band got its break, we would also migrate to the service entrance, where the monk was chained, and tease or talk to it.

"Well! One evening one of the band members said, 'Let's get the monkey drunk.' So they kept giving the monk all the beer he could drink (boy, that monkey could drink.) After a couple of breaks and a lot of beer, Dick came out to check his Baby and found the monk weaving all over the railing. Usually, a monkey has no trouble balancing himself when sober, but this poor monk kept falling off the railing.

"Dick really lost him temper. He approached the band and blasted, 'What son-of-a-bitch gave Baby the beer?' Well, nobody talked, naturally, and Dick carried the monk home to his cage. The funny thing about this is, the next morning when we were having breakfast, Dick didn't mention a single word about last evening's experience. That's how he was.

"Regarding Dick's companions: he seemed to be in the company of girls more often than men. On weekends, Friday evenings, Saturday and Sunday, we would have a great influx of out-of-town visitors. Among them came a beautiful girl – well proportioned – and her lover, a lesbian. When the band played, those two could always be seen dancing close together when they were not at their table drinking.

"This went on for a couple of weekends. I could see that Dick was very much attracted to the one beautiful gal. So, came the next weekend and the two gals showed up again. Now when the band took a break, somebody would put a nickel in the juke box so that they could continue to dance. The two gals in question got up and started dancing and eventually migrated to a dimly lit edge of the dance floor.

"By this time, Dick was vibrating with energy. He walked up to me and whispered 'Let's break them up.' So being young, foolish, and inexperienced I agreed for the hell of it. We approached the two gals, tapped them on their shoulders, separated them, and started dancing. The only trouble was I got the butch and he got the beauty.

"After a few dances, Dick and the girl disappeared somewhere, and left me with the square, heavy-set babe for twenty minutes or so. Surprisingly, there was no offense shown by the gal – she seemed to enjoy the experience – but when the gals left to go back to Chicago on Sunday, they never came back. Dick had a 'cat that swallowed the canary' smirk for the next few days. He would raise his eyebrows to me, but would say nothing. I understood only too well.

"On Sunday mornings, after breakfast, Dick and I would get into a row boat and skirt the shoreline around the lake, and guess who did the rowing? Dick would act out the part of an African missionary while I rowed and rowed. It was sort of a *missionary and African native* team. As our boat would approach groups of people, sitting or eating under a shady tree, Dick would get up to his full height, standing, and would pretend to open the 'good book' and proceed to preach. He would quote some of the passages of the good book and become a Hell and Brimstone preacher.

"When this happened, Dick would turn to me and say, 'Boy, let's move on to the next group of converts thirsting for the word.' By the time this every-Sunday episode would come

to an end, I was sunburned red, my back ached, and I had
water blisters on my hands to show for it.

"But now that I reflect on this experience, I wouldn't
have missed it for anything. Dick was truly an artist, always
practicing his art, and always perfecting it. The only regrets I
had about our experience together that summer was that all
good things must eventually come to an end, and end it did."

Baby wasn't Dick's only exotic pet. Aside from his two
Great Danes, he also owned a pet lion – though just for a
very short while. He saw an ad in a Chicago newspaper
offering a lion for $200 and immediately jumped into his limo
and drove to a house well out in the country. After meeting
the little old man who owned the beast, he watched as the
animal dragged its master through the house by its leash,
eventually arriving at Buckley. Almost at once the lion stood
on its hind legs, put its paws on Dick's shoulders, and licked
him. The sale was instantaneous. Dick put the huge creature
in the back seat of his limo and began to drive back to
Chicago.

Whether the lion misbehaved or Dick just began to
wonder what he'd ever do with the wild animal, however, he
changed his mind and returned the animal to its owner.

Buckley was ever the free spirit, ready to try anything
at any time. However, though his world remained as wild and

carefree as always, the outside world continued to change. Sooner or later the reality of that change had to penetrate even Dick's magical kingdom, and by late 1938 it did just that. The wild parties, complete with Angel lying naked in a coffin surrounded by candles, continued right until the end. His performances at the *Suzy Q* and *Planet Mars* still drew good crowds: a skit elegantly pantomiming an old man on a park bench drew raves. Without any make-up, using only his own malleable face and a subtle rearrangement of his suit jacket to create the illusion, he delivered a quaking, rattling monologue that captured the feel and look of old age precisely. But the walkathons were fading, and with them went a sizeable part of Dick's income and prestige. His parties began to cost more than he had, and for the first time since his childhood Dick Buckley was forced to ask for financial help from his friends.

Under the strain of his changing lifestyle, his relationship with Angel foundered and Buckley began to look outside of his beloved Chicago for new territories to conquer. A short stint on a cruise ship provided a change of scenery and apparently got him thinking of warmer climes once more, for in 1939 Dick made the move to Hollywood.

CHAPTER 4

Although the first rumblings of Nazi Panzer divisions were being heard throughout Europe, at home Americans were feeling a bit more confident about the economy and celebrated by flocking to theaters to watch *'Gone With the Wind'* and *'The Wizard of Oz.'*

Dick was just 33 and had already seen his meteoric star rise to the heavens and then cool. His talent was stronger and more original than ever, yet changing times and tastes momentarily left him a brilliant general without an army. For in Hollywood, although his name was still well-known from his walkathon appearances at the Polar Palace and elsewhere, names such as Gable and Bogart, and even his favorite, John Barrymore – all cast shadows long enough to eclipse a smaller star on the rise.

Luckily His Lordship found friends in Los Angeles, and moved in with one, Edward *Lord* Michaels, at the Hollywood Argyle Apartments.

"No sooner did he move in than it was a 24-hour open house," Michaels recalls. "Everybody was coming through all the time." A new coterie of friends was soon won, and the Buckley experience rolled ever onward with jazz and the inherent hip lifestyle as prime movers. "World shakers," as Buckley would say.

But Dick was involved in more than just the jazz world; his interests were as diverse as they were intense. History, philosophy, psychology, religion: without formal study, he managed to absorb an enormous spectrum of information and synthesize his own variations. Lord Buckley was a jazz thinker, without boundaries and unafraid of confrontation with the unknown. He jammed a hell of a life.

Within just a short while after moving to L.A., Dick landed a gig at *Charlie Foy's Supper Club*, bringing him instant status as a prodigal son returned. He met more beautiful women than he'd ever dreamed of, and was rarely at a loss for a lovely, talented escort. He and Betty Kean, a gifted dancer-comedian, dated for a time, but their relationship crumbled after a disastrous party at Betty's fantastic home.

Ms. Kean had just completed one of her first significant roles in a movie and the party guests included many of the cast and crew. After several drinks, Dick and Betty got into a major argument, and Buckley unleashed his sulphuric tongue to conclude the discussion.

When Buckley finally backed off and started to leave, several stunt men were sent after him to 'teach him some manners' in as disagreeable a manner as possible. Seeing the situation developing, Edward Michaels started in on Dick before the stunt men were able to make their move. Feigning a good old-fashioned wingding brawl, Michaels and Buckley battled out onto the lawn throwing vicious mock-punches and wrestling on the grass.

Their momentum took them out of sight of the surprised stunt men just long enough so Buckley could slip away unnoticed. He made his way to the house of another lady friend (on Western Ave.), cocky and secure in the complete success of his escape. But someone back at the party evidently second-guessed him, and the stuntmen arrived to carry out their instructions.

Dick had a show to do that night, and despite advice to the contrary, he appeared. "A normal person wouldn't have gone on and done the show, but he did anyway," Lord Michaels remembers. "He had one eye closed shut, he was bandaged and bruised – all beat up. He did an absolutely great show anyway… knocked everyone out."

Aside from his club work, Dick kept busy with one-nighters and benefits, seldom taking the time for a real vacation. But short-term adventures could hardly be avoided.

Just as '39 came to an end, Buckley and Lord Michaels were persuaded by a young friend to travel to Las Vegas as a team to rip off pin-ball machines by rigging them with piano wire, so they'd payoff at will. Buckley and Michaels were to be shields so that the pinball wizard could work his illicit magic. The idea was so bizarre that both Dick and his roommate agreed to go.

All went well for a while, until tallies of the food, drink, and hotel bills were compared with the trio's net receipts. Not surprisingly, the three desperados came out on the short end. In fact, they were so broke that only a miracle allowed them to get back to LA without skipping out on the hotel and borrowing gas money for the return trip.

Michaels was hanging out at the craps table watching Ramon Novarro and a big-wig from NBC shoot dice, when the NBC exec gave Michaels some money with the instructions "run it up." The dice were kind and his benefactor generous. Michaels took the $20 tip he received and quickly ran it up to $300 – just enough to cover the bills and get them on their way. The same night they got back to L.A., Dick did a show in which he improvised a blues number that told the entire story of their Vegas 'safari.'

When Michaels went into the Army three months later, Buckley returned to the road and out-of-town gigs. One of the first was in the spring of 1940, when he appeared at the *Strand Theater* in New York with the Carmen Cavallaro Orchestra – and an up-and-coming young singer named Perry Como, who'd just left the Ted Weems Orchestra. Dick concentrated on the four-person pantomime and his hat-switch routine, saving the hip material for after-hours with his friends.

His stately manner, dignified presence and tuxedoed appearance were not lost on New Yorkers, however. As a friend described it, "When he walked down Broadway, they knew he was around."

April 25-27 found Buckley in Hawaii playing the McKinley Auditorium with another up-and-coming young singer, by the name of Francis Albert Sinatra. Buckley and Sinatra hit it off, beginning a casual relationship that lasted for years.

But it was another chance meeting, this one in Chicago, that got Buckley back on track again, playing better shows and associating with a more distinguished circle of friends. At a party in his adopted home town, Dick met J.J. Levin, a promoter and manager who was instantly impressed by the Buckley magic. He agreed to manage Dick, and for the next five years while the world was at war, Sir Richard worked continuously in Vaudeville and at countless benefits.

In 1941, he travelled almost constantly, crisscrossing the country from N.Y. to L.A. with frequent appearances in Chicago and St. Louis. With the big-band era hitting its stride, Dick found himself on the bill with many good-sized orchestras – a change from the small jazz bands he was accustomed to working with.

At one such gig he was reunited with Fred Reczuch, who he hadn't seen since the summer of '38 at *Three Star Hennessey's*. "I was on my way to Southern California by bus," Fred recalls, "when I picked up a copy of the L.A. Times and there on the entertainment page was a big spread (ad) about the *Orpheum Theater*. They had vaudeville in those days, along with movies.

"Who do you suppose was appearing there along with Xavier Cugat and his orchestra? No one but Dick Buckley. Well! I could hardly contain myself, and I could hardly wait for the bus to pull into L.A.

"When we finally arrived, I found myself a hotel room, washed up, got dressed, and madly dashed to the *Orpheum*. It wasn't easy, since I was a total stranger, but somehow I felt like this was home since I had a friend I was about to see again.

"What a pleasant surprise. I finally found the theater in downtown L.A., went to the stage entrance, and there the doorman told me Dick had gone out to a telephone booth to answer a phone call. So, I took off again for this phone booth, and sure enough, there he was, back-to-me, talking a mile a minute but not aware that I was behind him. I decided not to interrupt his conversation, but would surprise him instead.

"I moved up very close to him, so that when he turned around he had to bump into me. When he finally hung up, sure enough he turned around without looking and practically knocked me over. He was shocked and started to apologize, when all of a sudden he recognized me, threw his arms around me, pumped my hand, and the first words he said were: "Why you old son of a bitch, what are you doing here? etc, etc."

"We visited off-stage about old times, and he finally asked where I was working in L.A. (music, naturally). When I told him all about my quitting the band business and working as an engineer, I think he was disappointed."

Dick was always dismayed to hear that one of his friends had 'dropped the calling' and left showbusiness. For no matter what venture a former performer got into, to Dick it was a sin to leave what he saw to be a religious endeavor.

Even in his daily life, Buckley couldn't help but perform wherever he was, whatever he was doing. On city streets he would flag down occupied taxi cabs, and on the premise he was a doctor or some other person in need of emergency transportation, hop in and hijack them to his destination. Or late at night, after his last show, he might walk up to a policeman, with a joint dangling from his lips, and describe the flight of a nonexistent 'drug fiend' with the exhortation that the cop drop everything and "pursue the villain." Such hijinks kept his friends shaking their heads and laughing, but luckily Dick's stage manners had improved to the point where Levin could get him bookings in top clubs. In December, 1941, Dick and Lord Jocko were playing the *Chase Hotel* in St. Louis, one of that city's best. A highly successful series of shows ingratiated them with the local upper crust, and they were repeatedly invited to luxurious homes and nearby ranches.

On Dec. 7th, when news of the Japanese sneak attack at Pearl Harbor reached them in St. Louis, the two men worked up a new act to express their patriotism and moral outrage. Lord Jocko bought Buckley several toy guns at a novelty shop, and with the band's drummer acting as a sound effects man, they incorporated the weapons into the act.

After announcing that the U.S. and Japan were now at war, Dick grabbed Jocko from the audience and accused him of being a Japanese spy – complete with taped eyes to distort their shape and an inverted cymbal to approximate an oriental hat. As *America at War*, Buckley shot his enemy first with a pistol, then a machinegun, and finally a bazooka. To no avail. Though the spy was bleeding profusely, (thanks to ketchup secreted in his hand), he managed to remain standing, bloodied but not bowed.

At this point, a pimp friend of theirs by the name of Blackie (aka "Mr. P.") suddenly appeared as a general to save the day. Blackie had begged Buckley for a moment onstage, and this was it. He walked briskly to the microphone, appearing every inch a gangster in disguise, and gave a loud Bronx cheer that immediately overcame the spy's last resistance. As Jocko fell to the stage, defeated by the quintessential American put-down, Buckley whispered: "Was it a mirage?" The audience went wild.

Despite his renewed success, or perhaps because of it, Dick went back to alcohol with a vengeance. Every day began with a stiff shot of gin, and before the day was through, he had imbibed more than his share. All too often, Jocko helped him to the bathroom where he would vomit the booze that had become a daily addiction.

Friends offered him marijuana as a superior alternative, and he received Prince Albert tobacco cans full of it. But although he was able to kick the habit for short stretches, drinking had   become an addition that wore at him from the inside and turned loose a wild, and sometimes vicious alter-ego.

When he sobered up, he was often remorseful for his actions under the influence, at times so much so that tears came to his eyes. But though the violence was tempered, the craziness continued.

One night not long after Pearl Harbor, "Mr. P" brought two of his lady friends, some pot, and champagne up to the suite where Dick and Jocko were staying. After partying a bit, Dick persuaded everyone to take off their clothes and take a shower. No one was about to turn down such an inviting offer, especially from Buckley.

So everyone squeezed into the tiny stall and got to know each other better. "Now the Three Musketeers are all here!" Buckley exclaimed, and the party continued.

From St. Louis, Dick went first to Chicago, where he appeared with Cab Calloway at the Sherman Hotel, and then to Las Vegas, where he played the El Rancho Hotel as an emcee and impressionist.   In addition to his Amos and Andy bit, he included a version of Louis Armstrong singing *"When the Saints Go Marching In,"* as well as several other short skits and stories.

While in Las Vegas, Dick somehow lost his draft card – at the time a serious offense. Temporarily jailed until they could determine if he had indeed registered, (he had, but was exempted), Buckley wasted no time organizing his fellow cellmates into a cohesive, productive group. When the jailer came to bring them their dinner, he found Buckley directing the men in a series of impromptu sketches.

By the fall of '42, Dick had made his way back east to Washington D.C., where he met O. O. "Bama" Merritt, who was to be friend, writer, and aide de camp for the next few years. They met when Don Donaldson, a mutual friend, came to Bama to buy some grass for Buckley.

"Who the hell is *he*?" Bama asked. "The most fantastic comedian you've ever seen," Donaldson told him, so he "rolled ten of the fattest joints ever" and set out to meet the man.

"We walked down to the *Windsor Room* where Buckley was appearing. He was on the bill with a trio, who moved off to the side and backed him when he took the stage.

"Well, I thought he was the greatest raconteur I'd ever seen in my entire life," Bama recalled. "I still remember what he did: *'Louis The Mouse'* and the *'Old Man.'* Eventually, he joined us at our booth and we took a walk around the block and lit up, and we came back and he went onstage – we were

all stoned on this grass, it must've been the greatest stuff in
the history of the world.

"But he did another set, just as if nothing had
happened, and when he got off, we went to the hotel Buckley
was staying at – the *Hotel Annapolis*. We had a few drinks,
talked, got high, and I gave him the rest of the joints.

"The next day he invited me to come see him at the
Capitol Theater. I was sitting in the front row, waiting for
something to happen, when suddenly I hear somebody
screaming: 'Hold it! I'm coming!'

"Buckley ran down the aisle, jumped over the
goddamn orchestra pit, and landed onstage. He always had to
run to the theater from his hotel, just making it every time.
The theater manager was always up in the air; the band never
knew if they should play his music."

Bama introduced Dick to two cute young ladies (Betty
and Betsy) who partied with them for several days, before
Dick moved on to New York. Apparently, he had told one of
the girls that he would be playing the *Strand Theater*, for they
followed him north. Bama was in the Big Apple on his own,
shopping for clothes, when he saw an ad proclaiming Dick's
appearance, and through the stage manager tracked him
down to the *Hotel Astor*.

"I got off the elevator, walked down the corridor, knocked on the door, and there were Betty and Betsy, stark naked. Buckley was in bed with a snake dancer and a twelve-foot cobra. He suggested that for safety's sake – having learned that the two girls were only 15 and 16 (though they looked older) – I take them home to my hotel. So, I did."

The foursome met every evening for dinner and conversation, until one of the girls was threatened by a woman for fooling around with her husband and both girls were sent on their way.

Buckley stayed in New York a while, working the *Strand* to capacity audiences. On Saturdays and Sundays, they'd play as many as seven shows to accommodate all the people, and Buckley usually stole the show. As one musician who was there, Jim Stutz, recalls:

"Musicians liked to work with Dick because his music was easy to play and there wasn't too much of it, so we could enjoy his act. What music there was, was of a swinging nature, but had to be rewritten so that it could be handled by the big bands because theater managers would complain that it would look funny to only have a few musicians playing while the rest of the band sat still."

One night, at a midnight show, it was standing room only – many of the audience members were servicemen and swing-shift factory workers who were taking advantage of the hectic show schedule that included up to seven performances a day. Even up in the balcony people were standing against the wall.

"He got these people up on stage and he realized they were very flexible, so he began to ad-lib and elaborate – even more so because of the full house. During the four-person act, the boy and girl on the end were getting eyes for each other and from his chair Buckley decided to develop the romance. He started throwing lines like, 'Are you married?' 'You're beautiful!' and got them so completely caught up with each other that in a few moments he had them embracing, finally kissing, and so fully engrossed that the audience was going wild, and they didn't even notice. Dick couldn't break the kiss up. When he stood up at the end of the act, the house went crazy."

When the long day of performances was over, Dick usually invited groups of friends and admirers back to his apartment to sit around on huge pillows, get high, and listen to his incredible stories well into the night. Unfortunately, on weekends the packed show schedule meant an early show on Sunday morning. After that first painful show each Sunday, the performers got a break, and, as Stutz describes, Buckley continued his personal performances.

"A group of us always got together after those early shows for a hearty breakfast at *Harry's Delicatessen*. We were pleased when Dick Buckley decided to join us, since it promised to make the occasion more entertaining.

"As we pushed open the door onto 48th St., we saw a lone figure approaching from the direction of Eighth Ave. We strolled slowly towards the Deli engrossed in our conversations and paying little attention to the approaching figure, until Buckley raised his hands and quietly said, 'Cool it. Watch this!'

"Keeping our eyes on Dick, we continued up the street until the young man came abreast of us. Just as we were about to pass the man on the walk, Dick stopped in his tracks, and raising his finger to point, said to him in a surprised tone, 'I say there, old man, how are you?' Naturally confused, the young man gave all of us a quick glance, but unable to avoid Buckley's engaging stare, he tried to find words to answer the unexpected greeting.

"Always quick to assess any situation, and even quicker to assess others and their thoughts, Dick lost no time in taking command of the situation, which, of course, he had planned all along.

"'What's your name again? No, don't tell me! Give me just a moment. I'll get it...'"

'This sort of thing continued for several minutes until Dick had very cleverly ascertained the poor yokel's name (for no native New Yorker would have been so easily taken-in) and was carrying the farce farther abroad by establishing names of mutual friends and incidents from the past.

"Soon, due to Buckley's friendly and convincing nature, the young man warmed to the situation, and, feeling more comfortable, became engrossed in conversation with Dick – now firmly convinced they had known each other in the past. However, as Dick continued to conjure up 'old friends' and happenings from the past, he began to allow an element of doubt to creep into the atmosphere. Recalling several incidents which the poor man was unable to recall, Dick began to shake his head.

"'Could I be mistaken? I was sure you were the same so-and-so... Oh, I'm sorry, please forgive me... I've made a mistake. I was sure you'd remember old Harry. Sorry to have inconvenienced you, old man.'

"And with that he walked off down the street."

Such persuasive powers awed Jim and his friends, who were convinced that Dick not only possessed a winning way and overwhelming spiel, but also "believed in the intricacies of ESP, clairvoyance, and mental telepathy, and practiced them regularly." Yet despite such a thorough knowledge of manipulative ways, Dick himself was surprisingly open to a good story.

Brett Howard, who hadn't seen Buckley since his walkathon days, met up with him again in Ohio in 1942, and proved Dick's susceptibility to a creative yarn.

"I was in Cincinnati. I had broken my knee and was on crutches, living at the *Cincinnati Club*. Doris Day was the lead singer, and I was in charge of her promotion. The big thing I was to do was to get personalities on the program.

"Who should come to town but the great personality Dick Buckley, who had now become *Lord* Buckley. So I called. You could imagine my reaction after carrying around this romantic illusion for all those years. So anyway, I said, 'You don't remember me, but I'm the mother of your child.'

"Well, he became fascinated, so he brought his business manager to be certain. He had laid so many girls in his Walkathon days that he wasn't absolutely sure I wasn't the mother of his illegitimate child. And in the meantime, I had invented the name of this child, and where it was and everything. It was just too funny. I got carried away because I was on crutches and everything.

"Well, he loved every moment of it. So we were going around then, me on crutches and him with his cape. And he was carrying a pipe. I remember smelling something and saying 'I think I smell pot.'

"'You *are* the mother of my child,' Buckley answered. It became the greatest line of my life. So anyway, this became a great romance. Christmas came and he was appearing in Detroit, still convinced ~~that I was the~~ mother of this child. It became an obsession with him. Which is hard to understand because he was so profligate. It was hard to believe he would even assume a responsibility like that.

"But he liked my mind, and he invited me up to Detroit. We were both staying in the same hotel – he had his room, and I had mine. His was a suite. He would get his paycheck, and I swear to God, he was making something like $1000 a week. And he was lucky if he had ten dollars left with all those people hanging around to get a handout. I mean, if you were really down and you had a scrawny beard and you were desperately in need for a fix of any kind and you'd crawled on your hands and knees to the back door of the theater, even if Buckley couldn't pay the bill for his hotel room, he'd give you ten bucks."

While staying with Buckley, Brett saw several of his shows and became convinced Dick's Amos and Andy bit was so effective it must be rigged. "He made me sit in the audience to prove to me that he had no connections with the people he had go up from the audience. He had that incredible power that... came straight from his eyes.

"I once asked him to explain how he managed to get people onstage, and he said, 'It's very simple. I look at you, I pick you, and you come with me. The day I can't do that, I'm finished.' And it was funny, they would come in gobs. Even when he was so drunk the theater-manager thought he couldn't go on."

Sober or not, Dick always managed to make his appearance. And he almost always managed to keep his sense of humor. When he found out Brett wasn't the mother of his child, he laughed.

Buckley's Royal Court was just coming into its own, a marvelous, fantastic world that His Lordship operated just within the bounds of what we call reality. Though he had acquired the title 'Lord' years earlier, it was only during the War years that a definite, stylized lifestyle came to represent his philosophy and demonstrate its tenets.

"If you call a woman a whore, she will behave like one; but if you call her a princess, she will become one."

Buckley called himself a Lord, and he saw that it worked in his life and in his profession, and he became one. Lord Buckley remained almost constantly busy during '42 and '43, appearing primarily in the New York area, but also in short bookings all over the country. It was in New York, however, that he met the attractive and well-connected Joanne Daun, who was to become his next wife.

Joanne was considerably younger than His Lordship, but completely captivated and devoted to his every whim. To catch his eye, she once followed him after a show wearing her mother's mink coat, with nothing on underneath. Needless to say, Lord Buckley noticed. It was through Joanne that Buckley first met Ed Sullivan, beginning an association and friendship that was to last until Richard's death. Sullivan was the toast of New York's columnists, and during the War he assembled troupes of performers to entertain at hospitals and military installations throughout the eastern U.S.

Buckley was an unselfish and willing participant in Sullivan's benefits, and in many others throughout the years, and both performers and servicemen were targets for his infectious energy and crazy humor.

One performance took His Lordship and a group of entertainers including Carol Bruce, and Lou & Florie Hammond, to the Norfolk Naval Station. At Norfolk, Richard couldn't refuse the temptation to include all the top brass in his Amos and Andy bit, including Admiral Nimitz. According to one troupe member, Lord Buckley received a standing ovation. "They didn't understand much of what he was saying, but they sure loved him."

On a flight to one USO show, Buckley was seated just behind Frank Sinatra and a priest who accompanied the show. All was quiet, with Richard engrossed in a book, until the priest bent over to tie his shoe. Seeing an opportunity, Buckley shouted loudly (presumably at Sinatra), "How dare you strike a man of the cloth?!"

As soon as everyone's attention was focused on the singer and the doubled-over priest, His Lordship went back to reading as though nothing had happened.

Between benefits and his vaudevillian appearances, Richard maintained the royal night life to which he had become accustomed throughout the years. At one wartime get-together, guests arrived at his apartment to find just one chair in the room – a high-backed throne chair – and large pillows strewn all about. Of course, His Lordship occupied the throne and his guests stretched out on the pillows.

With a clap of his hands Buckley summoned two 'harem girls,' who entered the chamber with great respect to answer their Lord's every whim. Of course, they were completely nude. "Slaves, fetch my very best hay," he intoned, and they backed out of the room to find a copper bowl filled with sticks of *tea*." The *tea* made the rounds, and everyone was soon floating on-high and listening with bemused fascination to Buckley's infinite variety of stories — both traditional and ad-libbed.

Not one to stop half-way, Lord Buckley also made clear an arrangement that allowed any male guest the opportunity to get to know his slave girls more intimately. As might be expected, however, there was a catch. If one of the men fell victim to the charms of the slave girls, his escort became Buckley's slave. In some instances, such an arrangement was highly regarded by both parties. In others, however, rather heated discussions developed, much to the amusement of the other party-goers.

Of course, heated discussions were a trademark of Buckley, although they were often extremely short and anything but sweet. Not long after he married Joanne, the two honeymooners were in the lounge of the *Astor Hotel* when Richard spied two Marines with 'fruit salad' on their uniforms standing at the bar. He watched them talk and drink for a while, and then walked up to the two soldiers with a slight smile of introduction. When he had captured their attention and they'd turned to meet him, he stopped and announced loudly, so all could hear, "You are two of the biggest shits I've ever met!"

Their reaction was quick and expected. After a terrible brawl, to Joanne's entreaties as to "Why?" he had taunted the Marines – especially knowing the many benefits he had performed for the military – Richard just shrugged and answered, "I wanted to see the looks on their faces."

In 1944, Lord Buckley appeared with Jane and Betty Kean, Ann Jeffries, and Dolores Grey in a revue called *'Fun for The Money'* in Los Angeles. He appeared in several sketches, with his *'Old Man'* bit earning him raves. The show ran about three months; when it closed, Richard worked clubs around L.A. doing the 4-person Amos and Andy routine.

Another Sullivan USO tour later in the year teamed Betty Kean and Buckley in a show that played a Richmond, Virginia military installation. In addition to Richard and Betty, several of the stars of the Olsen and Johnson show also appeared.

While flying to Richmond, Buckley lived up to his zany reputation by frightening the cast and making them laugh simultaneously. Since they were flying on an Army plane, smoking was forbidden. So when several passengers began to smell smoke, the alarm was quickly relayed throughout the cabin and the crew anxiously sought the location of the fire.

It didn't take long. His Lordship was discovered at the front of the plane blowing pot smoke at the pilot.

When they eventually landed, safe and sound, they were feted at a dinner and welcomed by thousands of servicemen who had been eagerly awaiting their arrival. Despite a highly successful performance, Lord Buckley was sent back after the show by train – where smoking, of cigarettes, was allowed.

Working with many of the greats of his era, (including Benny Goodman, Jimmy Dorsey, Duke Ellington, Louis Armstrong, Charley Barnet, Glen Gray, and many others), Buckley was once again on top of the world and making good money. When he travelled, he was always accompanied by a valet/aide de camp, and carried thirteen suitcases and two trunks to accommodate his huge wardrobe.

Early in 1945, Buckley played a gig in Washington D.C. where Mike Gould, then a song-plugger, spent a week with him. "I walked into his dressing room and stopped cold – there were only coat hooks in there, nothing else. Just as the show was about to start, in walked Buckley. He stopped just long enough to say hi, then walked right onstage and started his act. He walked out to the mike, very leisurely took out a cigarette, and lit it with a huge match.

"Then, just as casually, he blew the smoke into the spotlight, where the whole audience could see it. Now smoking wasn't allowed, so you could imagine the reaction when he does this and then says, "I bet every one of you would like to light up right now...Well, SUFFER."

Playing theaters on tour with the Woody Herman band, Buckley met Chubby Jackson, a bass player for the band. "Dick had a *cult* of friends who used to hang out with him, and he could always twist his commentary to break everyone up. He'd switch from a heavy British accent to a black dialect in a second, and both sounded like the real thing.

"Most of the time he was a wonderful guy to be around, but when he was drinking, he could punch someone out at the drop of a handkerchief. In fact, once he showed me teeth marks on his fist where he'd hit somebody.

"But the only time he ever got me mad was at the *Forest Hotel* in N.Y. It was the middle of the night, maybe 3 a.m., and we're all getting high, listening to music, and Dick's telling his stories. Steve Condos, the dancer, was there, and at the end of one of Buckley's stories he asked 'Do you want us to applaud?' Just joking with him. Well Dick got offended and started getting a bit salty. I had had enough and stood up to leave. But Dick blocked the door and wouldn't let anyone out of the room until he got his point across.

"Of course, on the other side of the ledger, he was always loyal to the little people, especially musicians. One time at a club on 52nd Street people were talking while the band was trying to play, and Dick got up, stopped the band, and physically threatened the audience if they kept on talking. It got pretty quiet."

Another fellow performer who met Buckley in '45 was actor Robert Mitchum, who went backstage after a show and found His Highness wearing jodhpurs and practicing with a whip for a story he was perfecting on the building of the pyramids. "He showed me a wardrobe trunk – it looked like a circus trunk – that was absolutely full of capes, crowns, all sorts of crazy things." To complete his wardrobe, and assist him in his new bit, Mitchum gave Buckley a pith helmet.

"Buckley was constantly affronted by life," Mitchum remembers, "and once admitted to being 'a master of self-deception.'" Nonetheless, Mitchum was a fan, describing His Lordship in glowing terms. "Onstage he was formidable, ten feet tall."

CHAPTER 5

In September of 1945, a chance meeting changed
Buckley's life. He had been signed to appear in a Shubert
revue called *"The Passing Show of 1946,"* starring Willie
Howard, Sid Ryan, and Bobby Morris, with "40 gorgeous
models" to enliven the scene.

One of these models, actually a dancer with
considerable training, was Elizabeth Hansen, a beautiful
blonde some twenty years Buckley's junior.

"The first time I saw him was backstage at the *Shubert
Theater.* I had been rehearsing in N.Y. for three or four weeks
for the *"Passing Show,"* and it was the night before we were to
leave for our opening date, which was in Hartford, Conn. I
had never seen him at the time, because he was a principal
and I was in the chorus, and in those days when you
rehearsed for a Shubert show you had to learn like twenty
numbers and end up doing twelve. It was a lot of learning to
do in a short period of time. This was in the fall of '45: Sept.
All I remember was that on the last night of rehearsing, I was

standing on stage, and this character kept looking at me, and walking from one end of the stage to the other, looking at me and walking back and forth. I asked someone, "Well, who is that?" I hadn't seen him around before, and you know how you ask, 'who's that, what do they do in the show?'...I could feel this person looking at me, beaming into me, and I wondered who is this? So, the next day we were on the train, and it was the first time I had toured with a big company like that.

"When I was 19 years old, I had been in NY and been studying, and I almost got into Milton Berle's Show, which was *'Springtime in Brazil,'* and I remember I was talking to Milton Berle, you know - we girls were auditioning for the show, and he was a very tall handsome young man, but he didn't move me at all. I mean he was Milton Berle, but I didn't think of him as being my type of gentleman. They took the show on the road and the show closed.

"Our show, *The Passing Show* with Willie Howard, was very successful. Willie Howard was a very famous Jewish comic: there were two brothers, and they played in vaudeville and legit theater. He was so little, His Lordship would call him 'the little mosquito' because he was so tiny, 5 ft 4. He was such a thin little man with this very big voice – he did cute little sketches, a very celebrated comedian, very famous. And

this was one of the last shows that he did. And then there was
Sid Ryan, a very famous musical comedian, and Masters and
Rolands, who were a brilliant dance team – did marvelous
satire.

"We all finally got on the train, and I'm sitting there,
and I don't really know anybody, because you've only known
one another for four weeks, and we're all rehearsing all the
time and everyone is very much their own person, and all of a
sudden here comes this cat up the isle, jazzing and singing,
and I'm wondering, 'Who in the world is this?' He's trying to
get everybody happy, and of course he's dressed just
exquisitely: gorgeous suit, beautiful shoes, wild beautiful shirt.
Then he had this gorgeous raincoat, you know, like James
Mason, had kind of a thing that crossed over and buttoned,
and then he'd wear this magnificent fedora, and he was the
only person in the show who had a valet. He had this very
proper gentleman, a negro, that sat just like he was in church,
with a black derby.

"It was in October we opened in Hartford; we had
three days there, and I always remember opening night. You
see, I was a dancer, and Mr. J.J. Shubert, who was the first
person I ever worked for in Detroit, had put me in the show.
I had gone to another audition, and I was late, I was always
late for everything in those days, so I was talking to this

fellow who I had gotten to know and he said 'gee, have you auditioned for *The Passing Show*,' and I said no, I hadn't even heard about it, and he said well come on, the Shubert office is right across the street, so go on over and see about it. I was starting another day, I knew where I was, so I went over there and just by chance Mr. Shubert was in, and for once in my life, I said the right thing. You know, you're scared to death, he's sitting there and he's one of the Gods of the theater, and I'm sitting there trying to be beautiful and impressive, and I said, "Don't you remember, Mr. Shubert? I worked for you in the *"Merry Widow"* in Detroit, Mich. He had picked me out of all the girls, I was fifteen at the time, and I had my hair in braids. I remember I washed it that day and I looked very Scandinavian, and he had asked me to go on the road to Chicago, but I had to refuse, because I had to go back to school. Anyway, he said 'Oh, Yeah!' and he was just delighted to see me again. And you know how you talk about scripts, well he said, 'Mitzi! Put her into the show. Get her into the theater immediately!' And suddenly I'm working; there's a contract. A show!"

"We opened in the *Bushnell Auditorium*, a big auditorium with beautiful dressing rooms and everything, and Shubert was a short little man who loved tall beautiful women and he always wanted me to be a showgirl – you see I'm 5' 7" and showgirls are 5'9" but if they needed a showgirl and the costume fit me, well, there I was. During a show there was always more material than they needed, and they would find out what they wanted to cut to fit the show. So between all the incomplete sets and havoc it's amazing what you had to do.

"I had to walk in high heels and I had a fish tail shirt with a train. I go walking up 16 stairs: I'm the top showgirl. I'm at the top and I have to kick this skirt behind me, and I suddenly realize I'm thirty-five feet up and there's nothing around me.

"The third night as we were closing, Lord Buckley asked me for a date. Well, I had about three offers for a date that night, and I said 'oh, well, alright' and he said he had a party of friends going out after the show and I thought 'where do you go in Hartford at midnight?' When you finish a show, you have to check in your make-up and your shoes – they take care of your costumes – and when you're not used to the routine it takes you awhile. So they had to wait for me. So I come down, and there I am, I have a skirt and sweater on and there he is with this party of girls. One in this gorgeous mink, jewels, and the whole bit, and I thought 'what am I going to do, I'll just have to rely on my fresh, youthful appearance.' (He was 20 years my senior.) And we get in this great big limousine and we drive off in the middle of nowhere and we go in and there's this swinging band and the place is jumping. We go in there and we are singing and suddenly we are dancing and we go over by the band, and everybody yells 'Hi Buckley! How are you?' We're out in the sticks – I mean, I'm used to New York City and everything seems like Squaresville – and all of a sudden everybody knows everybody and everything is very beautiful. But when we're going back in the cab, and he's drinking – he has this bottle – and he says 'let's go up to my hotel.' Well, I'd had a great time, but I don't want anybody juicing like this, so he's getting a little put-down and he wants to impress me and scare me a little and he takes and throws the bottle out the window.

"It didn't faze me at all. In fact, it was very funny. The cab driver asked us, 'do you mind if I pick up my girlfriend?'

"Well, we do, and this chick is sitting in the front and we're *battling* in the back and finally he drives me to my hotel and drops me off. I didn't even want to see this character again, so the next day when the chicks in the chorus line wanted to know what happened, I said 'forget it', I don't even want to see him. But I had to see him at the station. We were leaving and there he was in his raincoat, with a horrible hangover, and this was like, *forget it!* As far as I was concerned. I just looked at him and he looked so miserable, and I thought I never wanted to see him again, 'cause I was very young and I wasn't so impressed by the whole evening; it didn't mean that much to me then.

"He was like the third star in the show, so I'd always watch him and watch what he was doing. Of all things, I had to dress on the same floor as he did and I had to pass his dressing room every night. You can't avoid people, and we were one week there and we got very nice reviews and I was kind of drawn to him. I appreciated him as a talent. I was watching him as I was watching other performers, and I began to see that he was really a very polished performer.

"He was billed as Dick Buckley then, and he had gotten into the show through the auspices of JJ Levin, his agent, and it was quite a move for him in his career because he hadn't done legitimate theater before. JJ Shubert had seen him somewhere and had wanted him and it was a very nice thing for him even though he had to take less money: about $550 a week, when he'd been making $750 to $1250 in vaudeville. He'd worked steadily for five years without taking a week off, he told me, and spent it all. He had the most gorgeous wardrobe: he had seventeen pieces of luggage, 70 shirts, 500 ties, about sixteen suits and 32 pairs of shoes. It took a half a day to pack and half a day to unpack.

"We didn't speak at all in Washington, then we went to Philadelphia and it was kind of strange. I was watching him, seeing him more often."

He did his four-person bit, a dialogue in thick British accent with a young lady, and a donut sketch that Milton Berle had popularized. As usual, he was a tremendous success with the audiences, rivalling top-billed Willie Howard.

From Philadelphia the show moved on to Pittsburgh, with Elizabeth all the while maintaining her distance from the talented but outrageous Buckley. Their last night in the Iron City, Elizabeth and friends went out to the *Variety Club*, where who should they meet, but Lord Buckley. On his best behavior that night, Richard talked with wit and charm, and before the night was over, he invited her to the Musicians Club – she accepted.

That night, Buckley performed an impromptu John the Baptist bit and continued to impress Lizbeth with his talent and vibrant personality. The next day the show moved to Detroit, where their relationship began to flower into romance. The troupe got a week off for Christmas, and Buckley sent his lady-love a small ceramic skunk with a rose on it to invite her to Chicago where they could spend the holidays together. She accepted, and moved in with him just before Christmas.

In Chicago, Buckley was still king. Everybody knew him, everybody liked him. When he and Lizbeth would go out to eat at *The Pump Room* — one of Chicago's finest dining spots — they would literally be treated like visiting royalty.

As the new year began, Lord Buckley went on tour with the Woody Herman Band again, with Elizabeth accompanying him at shows all around the country. Their love had by then fully blossomed; they were virtually inseparable.

On July 23, Richard and Lizbeth were married in a Baltimore church. As "a salute to the beauty of our negro friends and to express the way we feel about racism," the ceremony was performed by a local religious leader, Rev. Body, a black man. Perhaps of even greater personal significance to Buckley, his best man (Don Donaldson) was a former KKK supporter whose past beliefs had changed so completely since his association with His Lordship that he showed no regret at the Buckleys' decision.

Lizbeth was dressed in a blue oriental outfit, Buckley a tux, and after the simple ceremony they went out to dinner. Afterwards, they just sat in a nearby park, talking and enjoying each other into the night. Their respite didn't last long. Nearly immediately they were back on the road to the Catskills, where they received the red-carpet treatment from

Grossingers and *The Concord*. Buckley, just turned 40, and his young wife were a classic couple, and their determination to stay in shape gave rise to the Buckley high-divers. No matter how cold the water, or how high the dive, Buckley was insistent about taking the plunge every day and Lizbeth never failed to follow. In fact, the two newlyweds seemed to be having so much fun, guests were often persuaded to join them in their merriment – even though water temperatures were often frigid!

Along with Lord Jocko and Olsen and Johnson, Buckley and Lizbeth greeted the return of the S.S. Randolph from the European War, appearing in a benefit the evening after they went to sea in a tugboat to welcome the returning soldiers. It was a time of great happiness, optimism, and renewed faith, for His Highness and the nation.

For the first time since his son's birth, Richard visited Fred and the boy's mother and stepfather, Paula and Tommy Russo. Even then, however, Buckley's true identity wasn't revealed to Fred until years later. During those first, tentative meetings, Richard was friendly but definitely non-committal. "I really didn't have any idea who in the world he was," Fred explained, "except that I always felt kind of strange when he was around. I suppose that's because we were never really introduced, and... he would come and if it seemed like it was okay he'd probably bring some kind of present for me, and then he would disappear and I wouldn't see him again for another year, or two, or three."

Lord Buckley's friend, David Hecht, had reappeared on the scene again after some legal hassles and a stint in the army. One of Buckley's first moves after meeting his old buddy again was to borrow part of his muster-out pay to buy Lizbeth a dress. Hecht wondered if possibly he should have waited a little longer to renew his acquaintanceship.

Living at the *Palace Hotel* on 49th Street and playing the famed *Latin Quarter*, life was good for the Buckleys. To be together more often, His Lordship included his bride in his act, as an assistant to bring him "My bonnet. My gloves. And my stick." After Lizbeth had walked onstage (wearing short-shorts and high heels) and delivered his requested items, he would announce "that will be all my little flower" and bow low as she left. Gazing after her with a smile and loving look he would add – to the audience – "Life can be beautiful." And he meant it.

Buckley's involvement in the jazz scene had expanded to include meetings with all the top musicians and friendships with many – including Charlie Parker. Lord and Lady Buckley often visited the nearby *Hurricane Club* where they watched and listened to the magical music of Louis

Armstrong, Cab Calloway, and Duke Ellington. Lord Buckley had appeared with nearly all the headliners, and frequently met them again after performances. Parker became a regular visitor to their home, and Lizbeth was once called upon to teach *"Bird"* how to dance ballet.

When the Buckleys strolled arm and arm through the city, as they did almost daily, they became local celebrities by virtue of personality as much as accomplishment. Buckley would talk to anyone, and everyone knew them and awaited their walks through Times Square. Their colorful appearance (Richard in tux or suit and Lizbeth in her short-shorts), their proudly erect carriage and energetic manner, even their smiles came to be welcomed trademarks.

Yet Richard wasn't always happy. His quicksilver temper, kept largely under control, still surfaced on occasion with customary violence. As it did one evening when a friend, Danny Elcheck, stopped in to visit. "Frank Cook had a pad right next to Lord Buckley, it was on the 12th floor, and there's a balcony. So Frank and I go over to Frank's pad and we *turn on* and get high there and we know Lord Buckley's next door 'cause we hear him. And so we decide to see what's happening over there, so we just step out this window instead of going around the hallway to the door. We just walk over and we sit down on the sill looking in, and Buckley's holding court and about eighteen or twenty people are there, and I'm just stoned out of my mind.

"So we're sitting there and Buckley had a habit like every now and then he'd tell a story and he'd pause, and nobody could interrupt or anything; then he'd go on and everything had to be done just this way. So he's telling this story, and then he pauses, and he tells the story, and pauses... and so finally you hear tokes and a minute goes by, and three minutes go by, and nobody says a fucking word. I don't know what struck me, but all of a sudden I say: 'Encore! Encore!'

"Well, that broke 'em all up, but Buckley really flipped and he came rushing up – it took three guys to pull him off me." But like nearly everyone who knew him, Elcheck forgave Buckley his vices for his virtues and remained friends with His Lordship. "Sometimes when I'd be alone with him, he'd still be *'on'* and I'd say to him, 'Look, you're talking to a hairy seaman – come down off the throne,' because, you know, he was never offstage – he was always His Lordship. But once in a while he'd just forget it, and that's how I remember him best."

By Buckley standards, the 1946 stay in New York was a lengthy one, and for a man who had been on the road nearly constantly for twenty years it was a welcome breather. But as friend and musician Mel Henke puts it, "There was no casual, relaxed atmosphere when Buckley was around." And so, he and Lizbeth were back on the road again by the Fall, with a mid-west tour taking them back once more to Buckley's walkathon stomping grounds.

In Minnesota for a show, he supervised the construction of a human pyramid of children. While all the kids were occupied as building blocks, Buckley secretly tied their clothes into knots. Appearing on the bill with a quick-change artist, he nailed the man's shoes to the floor. When he and Lizbeth went out for dinner at the fashionable *Flame Room*, he tipped the chef $10 before he ate, thus insuring complete culinary cooperation. He forcefully issued directives to everyone from maître d' on down, and the room was abuzz with the activity he generated.

Offstage, Buckley's hip translation of *The Nazz* was well-along in its evolution, but he kept such *good stuff* to himself and his close friends, believing, with good reason, that the rest of the world wasn't quite ready for it. Not even in New York, probably the worldwide center of hipdom, were the vibes yet right for such novel innovation.

New York. Alive and bustling once again after the war years, the names Joe DiMaggio and Joe Louis brought the long-repressed dreams of millions back into the spotlight. As

Blanche would say in *Street Car Named Desire*, "I don't want realism. I want magic!"

And Buckley was magic. Just walking in a crowd, he drew attention. One afternoon, he, Lizbeth, and Clyde Jones (of the Jones Brothers) were walking along through the throng at Coney Island. The sight of the statuesque blond and the black performer strolling together was most unusual for the time, yet according to Clyde, "everybody was staring at Lord Buckley, who was walking ten feet behind us."

Yet despite all his magic, His Lordship couldn't stop the clock. Vaudeville was terminally ill by 1947, the victim of changing tastes and a new invention called television. Friends of Buckley who were aware of the potential of the new medium advised him to make his move to the tube and cash in on its unquestionable possibilities. But Richard was still making a good living on the stage, and although he didn't doubt television's potential, he questioned his role in its future. For a while, TV was out.

But partying was not. In 1948 the greatest party of them all found a palatial home – just suited for a Lord and his glorious Royal Court.

CHAPTER 6

W. 71st St.

New York City.

It was meant to be.

Through a miraculous quirk of chance, Lord Buckley
and Lizbeth acquired the former personal hideaway of Mayor
Jimmy Walker, a large, distinctive, elegant apartment with a
hunchback midget for a gate-keeper, a fountain in the
entranceway, tile floors, and a high glass ceiling that extended
over the patio. It was classy. It was outrageous. It was vintage
Buckley. Yet, as attached as he quickly became to his new
home, he still had to go on the road occasionally to support
The Royal Court.

At the *RKO Dayton*, Lord Buckley emceed a show
featuring Dick Haynes and Evelyn Night, a stylish show
requiring a stylish performance. His "M' Lords and M'
Ladies" introduction certainly fit the bill, as did his black tux
and carefully-manicured appearance. However, after the
show, and after a few drinks, he invited virtually everyone

from the theater – including the theater manager – to accompany him to a nearby club where his friends Foster and Bobby Johnson were appearing. And the results were anything but stylish.

The show was at a large "colored club," with most performers, employees, and patrons being black. Some 400 people were enjoying the performance, when in strolled Buckley, followed by nearly twenty friends from the RKO. After he had made sure they were comfortably seated at a long table directly in front of the stage, His Highness went backstage to visit and treat friends and fellow performers to a toot and toke. When everyone was feeling just right, and a break came in the flow of the show, Richard was asked to perform. Never one to turn down an opportunity to appear before an audience, His Highness accepted readily and went on in an instant.

His performance that night was both powerful and impactful. "*Sweet Georgia*" was the theme music for a dramatic story of racial tensions culminating with a black man being hanged. The tension inside the club was palpable. Some people applauded wildly, others stared in shocked or confused silence. Buckley, satisfied by the cheers and feeling frisky, returned to his table, lit up a stick of *tea*, and puffed away as though everyone else was foolish for not joining him.

Unfortunately, the RKO theater manager's wife was seated directly across from His Highness, and she crinkled up her nose. "What on earth are you smoking?"

"Madam," Richard replied, "I don't ask you what you're doing, and I'd appreciate the same courtesy."

She was not in such a polite mood. "If I'd known you were this sort, I would have never accepted your invitation," she sniffed, and it was just enough to truly piss Richard off.

Unzipping his fly under the table, he let her have it. As she realized just what was happening, she screamed... and her husband went berserk. Several waiters quickly stepped in to squelch the chaos, presented His Highness with the bill for the group, and invited them all to leave.

Confronted with a bill for twenty guests, Richard looked the waiter bravely in the eye and casually announced, "Sorry old chap, but I don't have a dime on me."

Foster and Bobby were fired immediately, with the management attaching their salaries to pay the tab of the RKO group. Working his way through the crowd, Foster interceded with the bouncers and Buckley left without the seemingly inevitable confrontation. The next day, Lord Buckley reimbursed the two dancers the entire amount, and incredibly enough finished out his gig at the RKO.

That same week, Foster went with Buckley to a fire sale at an appliance store, where Richard picked out a television and a record player and shipped them back to N.Y. A few weeks later he met up with Lord Buckley back in the Big Apple, and found the TV and record player had been gutted and the boxes used as flower pots.

Regular visitors to his 71st St. apartment, the duo went out to have lunch with Buckley one afternoon at a respectable N.Y. café, and His Lordship ordered steak from the uniformed, middle-aged waitress. While they waited for the meal to be prepared, Buckley sat quietly and discussed a variety of topics in hushed tones befitting the toney cafe. But when the steak was put down in front of him, his reaction was immediate and anything but sedate.

"What is this, a steak or a burnt sacrifice!" he bellowed as he jumped up, and instantaneously the restaurant was in an uproar. When everything was finally adjusted to his approval, Lord Buckley sat back and explained with a smile, "I do love to shake them up."

At one gathering at the 71st St. apartment, His Lordship invited a large group of circus performers, along with musicians and other entertainment people including Sid Gould and Larry Storch. The party was wailing away into the wee hours of the morning when a voice came at the door to *'stop all that noise.'* Lord Buckley, dressed only in his shorts, stepped indignantly out into the snow to challenge his critic to "send ten cops – I'm ready for them."

A short while later, two policemen *did* show up, and Buckley graciously invited them in. After they had asked him to lower the commotion just a wee bit, they turned to find Richard blocking the door.

"A tumbler of Scotch for my guests," Buckley bellowed, and before the confused officers could figure out what was happening, they were each handed a tall tumbler of Scotch. "Drink up chaps. No hard feelings," His Lordship graciously conceded. The policemen were hesitant to join the revelry, but His Highness was not to be denied. Through a skillful combination of persuasion and veiled indignation he cajoled them into draining their drinks, and then sent them on their way and resumed the party – at full volume.

A few weeks later, Larry Storch accompanied Lizbeth and His Lordship on a gig up to the Catskills, where Buckley was booked to play *Grossinger's* – one of the best-known clubs in the Borscht Belt. Riding in a '48 Buick, with Richard in his customary classy duds and Lizbeth adorned in "an outfit that made her look to be an Oriental princess," the threesome drove all the way up into the mountains with spirits and hopes running high. But 90 minutes in front of an elderly

Jewish audience shattered any illusions of his customary success. Although a few people in the audience were totally captivated by his Amos and Andy, the vast majority couldn't understand the black dialect and failed to grasp what was happening. As far as they were concerned, it might have been Chinese pantomime.

On the way back to New York, Richard was seething. "Those peasants!" he fumed, "they didn't even appreciate what they were missing!" As the drive got longer and longer, and the mood darker and darker, the three decided it might be a good idea to stop at a roadside pub and unwind a bit before continuing.

The Never Sink Inn was fairly crowded that evening, and conversation was lively. The entrance of Buckley & Co. certainly stimulated that atmosphere. When they had established a place at the bar, Lizbeth asked her husband what he was going to speak about and Richard suggested *Communism in China*. His Lordship struck an orator's pose, but the conversations continued.

When it became clear the crowd wasn't about to give His Highness the floor without some prompting, Lizbeth stepped forward.

"Quiet!" she screamed. "Richard is going to talk about China and he earns more in one week than you do in a year!"

Most of the group got the message, but one woman was neither impressed nor curious and continued to chat merrily away. Buckley suffered her chatter for just a few seconds, before rendering his opinion of her human condition.

"You, madam, are an *idiot*," he announced matter-of-factly.

Her conversation stopped abruptly, but His Lordship's satisfied sigh was interrupted by the sound of the woman's husband getting up from his stool and stretching his mammoth frame skyward. Buckley had to look up to apologize.

All was smoothed over, with some difficulty, and all returned to normal. Buckley began to speak again... and the woman returned to her conversation. As he continued his lecture, it became more and more obvious that he wasn't going to be able to hold himself back and, sure enough, he couldn't. The woman's "drivel" drove him over the brink.

"I apologize if I repeat myself," he said to her sweetly, "but I'm afraid I must reiterate: Madam, you are an idiot!"

This time her husband wasn't alone. The whole bar came after them, but they weren't quite fast enough.

"Lord Storch," Buckley commanded as he turned, grabbed Lizbeth, and headed full stride for the door, "don't pay for a thing!"

*****

Back in New York, the 71st Street hideaway continued to be ground zero for some of the most talented and unusual characters in the City, the home of the Royal Court. Lizbeth continued giving ballet lessons to a wide variety of students, with Buckley as their most severe critic. While Lord Storch was doing his best to find the rhythm of the dance techniques, Buckley lay on a couch adjacent to the workout area and laughed playfully. "You'll never make it, Your Lordship," he'd decide, only to be contradicted gently by his wife, who maintained – with reservations – that *all* her students could make it.

When the Jones Brothers stopped in during the midst of a tour unannounced, Buckley welcomed them as if their arrival was long expected and immediately ushered them in for breakfast. Lady Buckley, always the perfect hostess, made the men comfortable while His Lord- ship called the neighborhood butcher and put in an order for "four or five dozen of your finest little pigs." When the sausage arrived, a hearty meal for all was whipped up in the kitchen and served to the group seated in the living room listening to Buckley's tales and telling a few of their own.

His Lordship's generosity was often repaid – usually in the form of a loan or gift – but occasionally he balked at accepting anything other than thanks. For instance, when he played the RKO Boston later in '48, the Jones Brothers were delighted to learn he was in town and hurried over to greet him. Herb went backstage after a performance and was royally-received, but when he invited His Lordship to his home, Lord Buckley declined with his usual aplomb.

"My dear Lord Jones, I must decline the invitation on the grounds that I'd seduce your daughter, your wife would run after me, and your son would never forget me."

With more than a hint of truth to his humor, Herb didn't press the point.

Buckley continued to perform his Amos and Andy routine at most gigs, though the hip translations were becoming increasingly dominant in his thoughts and off-stage performances. The times were a-changing, and Buckley was determined to lead the change as he always had. But booze remained a critical stumbling block to His Lordship's career and private life, transforming, as it did, a brilliant performer and respected gentleman into a raging alcoholic who resembled Lord Buckley in physical appearance only.

During one night on the town, Lord and Lady Buckley were partying with George Raft and others when His Lordship decided he wanted to socialize with several old friends he spied in the club. Leaving Lizbeth and Raft to talk, he set out to shake some hands and swap stories. Unfortunately, his *brief* sojourn stretched interminably and Lizbeth was unable to strike up much of a conversation with the taciturn Raft. Finally, unwilling to wait any longer, Lady B. stormed out of the club and walked home.

It was quite a while later when Buckley returned home, drunk and angry. His temper was matched, however, by his wife's, and when the dialogue reached the boiling point, Lizbeth reacted in the most appropriate way she knew how – she smashed his prize bottle of Scotch.

Buckley was furious, and Lizbeth wasn't about to wait around for his next move. She scampered to a safe hiding place and remained secluded until Buckley's fury died and he passed out on the bed. The following morning, he apologized.

Incidents such as this, and a growing reputation among club owners and agents that Buckley was difficult, finally persuaded His Lordship to try AA – Alcoholics Anonymous. With the zealous enthusiasm he devoted to all his efforts, Buckley determined to "stamp out this oily, rotten stuff."

Replacing alcohol with pot, His Highness's hip consciousness
soared, and both the Royal Court and his professional career
soared with it. Secure in a real home for the first time ever,
Buckley entertained everyone from Ed Sullivan to strangers
he met on the street at the 71st Street apartment. Lady
Buckley served elegantly as First Lady and Hostess of the
Court, a most remarkable task considering His Lordship
brought guests unexpectedly at all hours of the day and night
on a regular basis.

Among the newfound friends His Lordship brought
back to the apartment was Ben Lassiter, called Tex, a skilled
master electrician who had worked seagoing vessels for years
until his drinking landed him at the Bowery AA – where he
met Buckley. Lady Buckley accompanied His Highness to the
Bowery meeting place, and remembers Tex as a tragic
paradox. "We met him at the Alcoholics Anonymous
meeting, and Lord Buckley insisted we bring him home.

"Well, here I was, a young bride from Minnesota, and
Tex was a big burly seaman – in fact, he looked a bit like His
Lordship. But to me he just looked like another down and
out drunk. Lord Buckley saw something in him, however, and
he convinced me to bring him home. So we brought him
back to the apartment, put him to bed, and covered him up
with blankets. All the while, he doesn't say a word. When he

woke up the next day, he told us he thought he'd died looking up at the glass roof and down at the terra cotta floor.

"Well, he still didn't talk much, but His Lordship invited him to stay as our guest. Lord Buckley told him they could help each other beat the booze. So he did, and he turned out to be a great worker: he fixed our couch, 'swabbed the decks', washed the dishes, painted the kitchen, and much more. After a while he came into some money and he bought us an old, out-of-tune player piano that he insisted we keep. In fact, it was so out of tune that it was rarely played. The only time it really sounded good was when Lord Buckley brought home a little old lady he'd met during his rounds – we called her Madame Pumpernickel – and she played for us – beautifully. Anyway, Tex finally thought he was strong enough to move out, but when he called his wife back in Virginia, from whom he'd been separated for twelve years, he found out she'd remarried and he started drinking again. We got him to a hospital to dry out, but eventually we moved and lost track of each other."

Buckley's attempt at revitalizing himself was not lost on those in his profession. The Edward Sherman agency in N.Y. was impressed enough by the new Buckley to book him for the next three years, and with numerous friends among musicians and other performers, Buckley was constantly in demand.

Perhaps it was fated that such a positive change be reflected in other areas of his life as well. In any case, October 1948 saw Lizbeth pregnant with their first child, and the Royal Court prepared to welcome a prince or princess into its midst.

Good tidings at home were matched by successes on stage, including a *Comedians' Night at the Copa* in which Lord Buckley closed a show that featured Joe E. Lewis, Milton Berle, George Burns, Henny Youngman, and Jack E. Leonard – the best of the day. According to friend and fellow entertainer Foster Johnson, "After everyone else had done their bit, Dick came on and it was as though they hadn't even appeared. He captivated the audience. With his extemporaneous kibitzing, he *became* the show as soon as he appeared."

A few months later, at a benefit for the Heart Fund at the *Copacabana*, Lord Buckley joined Ethel Merman, Earl Wilson, Kate Smith, Lee Tracy, and dozens of other celebrities in a gala evening of entertainment. Ed Sullivan served as emcee, and once again His Lordship was saved for last. Dressed elegantly in tails, Buckley came on after Kate Smith's *"God Bless America,"* a difficult act to follow. But, rising to the occasion, he selected Merman, Tracy, and two other celebrities to join him for the 4-person pantomime, and winged one of his finest, and best-received performances ever.

Walking home that night, he and Lizbeth floated "on feathers and clouds" over the tumultuous reception, and the Royal Court hummed with joyous intensity for weeks.

Discovering that old friend and associate Lord Jocko was working *Hurley's Log Cabin* in the City, Lord Buckley and Lizbeth went to pay him a visit. They found Jocko working to a boisterous crowd of thugs and drunks, playing much of the old Chicago schtick as a regular featured performer.

Buckley and Lady B had barely arrived in the smokey confines of the club when an argument between a hooker and her pimp exploded into a gun battle in which a stripper was shot and Jocko was hit in the leg by a ricochet. After the disturbance died down, and Jocko bandaged his wound, Buckley offered Jocko a gig touring with him as his valet. After an initial refusal, Jocko reconsidered and accompanied him on tour with the Woody Herman Band.

Near-constant association with the greats of jazz kept Buckley's hip act polished and alive, but club owners were only interested in the old, proven material, not some radical new approach. In '48 Lord Buckley was not to be denied,

however, and for the first time he tried his *"Hipsters, Flipsters,
and Finger-Popping Daddies"* translation of Antony's speech at
the death of Caesar. Although he wowed the bands in the
small nightclubs he performed in, most of the audiences were
left completely in the dark, unable to even recognize many of
the words and phrases. After several attempts, owners
insisted he return to the Amos and Andy routine and forget
the hip stuff. Disappointed but undaunted, Lord Buckley
continued to entertain his friends with the translations while
sticking to the standard bits for the masses.

Between road-trips with big bands and extended gigs
at the *Palace* and other top N.Y. clubs, Buckley was not only
working regularly but making good money and spending it
freely. His Lordship and Lady B could often be seen walking
the City streets in their elegant regalia, and it wasn't at all
unusual to see Richard start up a conversation with a frisky
squirrel or bellow a greeting to a flock of pigeons while
shaking his cane to get their attention.

Guests to his home could expect a warm welcome and
a wide variety of off-beat characters, though regular visitors
were expected to "pay homage" to his Lordship by bringing
something to help maintain the Court. The gifts were usually
inexpensive but practical, more a demonstration of good faith

and a cooperative nature than anything else. Food, drink, pot
– it mattered not.

New members of the Court were frequently
commanded to perform for the assemblage, with their talent
both a contribution and a confirmation of their willingness to
participate in the world Buckley created. Somewhat ironically,
although His Lordship was unquestionably in command of
the situation – whatever it might be, he elevated a very few
select figures to the rank of King, including Ed Sullivan.

However, now even a King can always command his
Queen, and though Lizbeth was usually Buckley's most
willing subject, on rare occasions he bowed to her objections
– if they were strenuous enough to overcome his inherent
self-assurance. Such a situation developed while Lizbeth was
pregnant with their first child, and Buckley reacted with first
anger, then shocked indignation, and finally resignation.

In was early 1949, and the Buckleys were entertaining a
group of fellow entertainers and their wives, including Bobby
and Foster Johnson and several others. At one point in the
proceedings, Buckley was suddenly seized with an idea for a
happening, and asked his guests to step out onto the patio for
a few moments while he arranged the episode. Everyone
cooperated and went out to wait by the fountain in anxious
anticipation of Lord Buckley's summons to return.

When the summons finally came, Buckley seemed sullen and irritated, and as soon as the guests moved back into the main room His Lordship immediately explained the reason why. It seems he had planned to stage a scene in which Lizbeth reclined nude on the couch while Bobby Foster's wife played a handmaiden and sat on the floor massaging Lady Buckley's stomach. Lizbeth had flatly refused, and he was unable to sway her. After calling her a series of names — some quite imaginative — he concluded his tirade with an observation that summed up his disappointment:

"Women," he groaned, "they become involved in your life but refuse to accede to your wishes."

Lizbeth became even more upset with his pronouncement, and the Court seemed ready to adjourn for the night. But as quickly as the disagreement sprang up, it disappeared, as Buckley went into a corner and sat by himself to portray a Chinese character in meditation. In a few moments, the party continued.

With all the fun and excitement of those times, June 30, 1949 stood out as a special day for even the most surfeited member of the Royal Court. For on that day Lizbeth gave birth to Buckley's first daughter, named Laurie by Ed Sullivan, and the Court celebrated the long-awaited addition to the royal family in a variety of ways, not all of them strictly legal. But Laurie's presence probably contributed as much to His Lordship's growing maturity as his AA membership, yet neither interrupted the continuity of the Buckley social scene.

If anything, Richard and Lizbeth became even more protective and supportive, as illustrated in a confrontation between George Von Physter and Lady B at a 71st St. get-together. Von Physter had been dubbed "The Reluctant Duke" because of his reluctance to perform for His Highness, and nothing anyone could do could change his mind. Buckley, of course, was most persistent in his insistence that George do *something*, but to no avail. "He was leaning on me this one night," Von Physter recalls, "doing everything in his power to make me perform. But I wouldn't do it. I absolutely refused. Finally, after raising hell for the longest period of time, Buckley got me so infuriated, that I jumped up and decided that I was going to punch him out. But when I ran after him, Buckley ran into the bathroom and locked the door.

"I was so mad, I was going to kick the door in, when I stopped for just a second and looked around and saw this female, healthy as a bear, with legs like iron, coming down that hall like a panther. It was Lady Buckley. I took one look at her, hesitated just an instant, and then turned and ran – not only into the other room, but out the front door and into the street. She scared the shit out of me! She's dedicated, a magnificent broad I tell ya!"

Aside from intimidating Buckley's attackers, Lizbeth was the behind-the-scenes mastermind of the household. To maintain the image of a spotless castle, and fulfill the on-the-spot demands of His Lordship and the multitude that comprised his Court, Lizbeth kept up a killing pace that often matched, and occasionally even surpassed Buckley's. Meals were always designed to accommodate anywhere from the immediate family to several dozen with a quick shift of the menu, and Lizbeth even studied under professional chefs His Lordship brought home to learn their culinary secrets.

It was never a surprise when Richard brought home guests, no matter if it was just a new-found friend, a needy soul he bumped into on the street, or considerably more. After a performance in *"Holiday in Paris,"* in which Lord Buckley was featured, he brought home a thirty-man negro choir; Lady B. made do as best she could.

Professionally, Lord Buckley was making good money but suffered through the ups and down of attempting to open a new frontier in the entertainment business. The hip material was still frowned upon, and even his regular act didn't always hit the mark – at least not immediately.

Playing the *Adams Theater* in Newark – a tour theater in a tough neighborhood – His Lordship had the misfortune of following an extremely attractive young woman on the bill. When he came out, dressed immaculately in tux and tails, ("looking like a cat from another time and space," according to RCA producer Jack Lewis), the audience began to boo spontaneously, not even allowing him to begin his act. For ten minutes Buckley endured their displeasure, but finally he won them over and turned their boos to applause. No sooner had he done so, however, than he stared at the crowd intensely, leaned up close to the microphone, and said ever-so-sarcastically, "You're all *diseased.*"

With that he walked off. The applause roared for ten minutes, but he wouldn't come back. He had offered them better than they deserved, and now they knew it. His satisfaction was complete.

No more so, however, than when he played a benefit gig a few months later for drug offenders in Lexington, Kentucky, a show that began with such an unusual reception that Buckley incorporated it into one of his tall-but-true tales. At meetings of the Royal Court he would lean back in his throne chair, expel a long sigh of thoughtful readiness, and recite with his powerful, hypnotic voice:

"Lexington, Kentucky. I was playing the *Ben Ali Theater* there, and I called the warden at the rehabilitation center for the *lustres of life,* the narcotic division, as it were. So I called up the warden and said, 'Hello warden, this is Lord Buckley. I'm down here at the *Ben Ali Theater* and I appreciate the magnificent work you've been doing for the noble lads and lasses, and I know that you are cognizant of the power of laughter and therapy, and I should like to do a concert for you.' He said, 'Oh, very good, we'll send down Dr. Thorpe.'

"So they sent down the good doctor, who turned out to be a very astute gentleman in an advanced automobile and thick glasses, and for the four miles from the theater to the rehabilitation center I was interrogating him with a nervous but balanced rhythm 'porcupine' interrogation to find out exactly what was taking place at this organization. What was curing, and what wasn't curing, and the many, many silent definitions of the problem.

Dick Buckley in Chicago

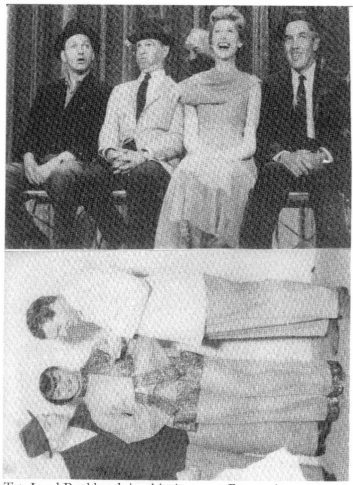

Top: Lord Buckley doing his 4-person Pantomime on
Ed Sullivan Show

Bottom: Buckley with fellow performers

Lord Buckley with Ed Sullivan

Lady Buckley

Milton Berle (l) and Buckley during Walkathon

"I found out they were using everything... but love.

Love – shone, projected, manifested – love of humanity.

Those people were giving evidence in great beauty to the

second greatest word in the world, which is SERVICE. By

gads!

"So we went in through the large gate – clang, clang –

and walked down three flights of stairs to a 1500-seat theater.

In the 1500 seats were seated 1500 of the WILDEST cats you

ever laid your eyes upon in dis here born world. They were

magnificently alerted, but starving for *love*. So I walked

backstage and a large fellow in his white coverall said, 'What

kind of music would you like, sir? Would you like bee-bop,

classical, semi-classic, modern, jazz?... JESUS CHRIST

BUCKLEY, don't you remember me? For Chrissake I used

to play for you at the *Suzy Q*! What do ya say, Daddy?' He

patted me and I fell into his arms and another fellow came

walking by and said 'Hey Buckley, how you doing?'

"So I took three steps out on the stage – bzzzt. And I

took another step – bzzzt. And I got to center stage and what

sounded to me like at least 900 of these people, in my sound

calculator   of the reaction of the dimension were saying, 'Hey

Buckley! How's it moving Buckley!'

"Now the movement was so strong it was like I had

my head down and I couldn't get my head up. Believe me,

this was most profound, and I'll tell you why. It was the sound of a lot of wild birds in a glass cage looking out and seeing another wild bird on the limb."

Thoroughly motivated by the sight of all his old friends and associates, Buckley launched into his *'mass pantomimicism'* with zest. "It was a glorious bouquet," His Lordship recalled. "The music followed my every rhythm and the people were divine.

"Excited, I wanted to say something gracious, or beautiful. But I didn't take enough tempo to prepare the search of the thought for that beauty, you see. As a consequence, I wound up saying,

'Ladies and gentlemen, many, many years ago, Confucii - the ancient precious sage of the world's best-known and oldest civilization, the Chinese, once called his favorite students beneath the beautiful warm bell of the cherry trees and said to them, *'Len-go he, sa hoo do zi hytimooa, zhaoo doi doi dom.'* Translated, it means briefly, 'If you get to it, and you cannot do it, there you jolly well are, aren't you.' And they flipped, and I flipped."

As Buckley was about to leave the Center, he was told a story by Dr. Thorpe concerning an inmate who was just leaving the facility for the fifth time. As Buckley described it, "He was riding the horse, a very difficult beast. Heroin they

call it; 'horse' is the trade name for the beggar. Once you
mount the fellow, you can't dismount. There you go, hill and
dale. And by Jove, whenever the horse gets hungry it'll tear
up the mountain to get some grass, or something to nibble
on.

"So this chap had left five times – without love
though, the therapy wasn't there; everything but love was in
the treatment you see. Love cannot be shammed, cannot be
camouflaged. It must be there. So Dr. Thorpe said to him,
'This time, when you go out, you're not going to use the
needle, are you?' This fellow looked Dr. Thorpe fair, square-
beamed in the eye and said, 'Dr. Thorpe, will a bear shit in
the woods?' Now obviously, a bear cannot do his business at
5th and Main, 'cause he'll attract a large crowd; he can't do it
on Highway 61, they won't allow him in any of the service
stations; he can't do it on the reservations; he *must* shit in the
woods."

Buckley did omit one short segment of his visit. As he
was leaving, several inmates came up to His Highness and
asked him for sticks of gum – which were not permitted in
the facility. Buckley didn't have any gum, but a friend who
had accompanied him, Lord Cyrus, was holding several sticks
of *tea*. So as they left, Cy dropped the joints into the bushes
that fronted the building while Lord Buckley strutted

elegantly on ahead with Dr. Thorpe, chatting intently to divert any inquisitive eyes. The only ones to see were the inmates, and they kept the information to themselves.

Such benefit performances were second nature to Buckley, and extended throughout his career. While many performers had donated their time to entertain the troops during WW II, His Lordship continued his appearances at military bases and hospitals across the country. 'Bama, Dave Lambert, and Buckley appeared in several Red Cross shows just as the Korean War was heating up, and as usual were treated with tremendous respect and admiration by the servicemen. In fact, after one show just outside N.Y.C., the soldiers thronged around Buckley and company so enthusiastically that it took over an hour for them to leave the auditorium.

In April, 1950, Lizbeth and several of His Lordship's friends planned a 44th birthday celebration for Buckley, a party that turned out to be a howling success. As the more than 200 guests arrived, Buckley personally advised them not to throw up on the glass roof that extended out over the patio. "I just finished cleaning it on my hands and knees," he explained.

Virtually everyone brought a bottle to the occasion, and a good many brought a variety of other party stuffs to

boggle the mind. Lizbeth and friends had arranged the food
and layout, and Buckley's new manager, George Greif,
supervised the liquor.

Buckley, of course, supervised everything.

The party began on a Friday night and continued
uninterrupted straight through til Sunday – less than twenty
guests left in the meantime, although a sizeable number were
overwhelmed by the duration and intensity of the celebration
and passed-out where they sat.

"Set the body over there," Buckley ordered regularly
throughout the two days, and the nearest member of the
Court would drag the unconscious reveler over to a relatively
sedate corner and prop him or her up against the wall to
recuperate.

After one particularly intense period, in which the
normally crazed atmosphere became even more exotic,
Buckley led a large group out to the fountain to present one
of his impromptu happenings. The crowd was ready for
anything, and they got it.

Improvising an entire Italian opera, Lord Buckley
played all the characters with a gusto and zest that enthralled
his audience even though they had little idea what he was
singing about. "It was as though he had a writing pad in his
mind," was the way one guest described it, and for nearly ten

minutes the presentation flowed as though scripted. Finally, a character called out "Sissilito," apparently summoning another cast member, and Buckley pulled down his zipper and introduced the new member.

Pandemonium broke out. People screamed, felt into the fountain, smashed glasses. Buckley, always the consummate actor, fell to the floor as though dead, but watched the crazed proceedings with a satisfied smile on his face. Once again, he had *SHOOK* them.

Those in attendance who didn't already know were pleasantly surprised to learn that Lizbeth was pregnant once again, and others who were totally out of touch saw the infant Laurie for the first time. Completely at ease in the midst of the maelstrom, the baby slept peacefully at regular intervals, and seemed to adapt to the proceedings with royal forbearance.

Buckley worked almost exclusively in and around New York in 1950, but occasionally gigs took him elsewhere and involved him in all sorts of other endeavors. In Boston for a gig at the RKO, Lord Buckley became acquainted with the Yakus Brothers, whose recording studio was the site for the first professional Buckley recordings since he produced a sleep aid '78' in the early 40's. Backed by a jazz band, His Highness did several of the new, hip bits he had been

working on, including *"The Nazz"* and *"Hipsters, Flipsters..."*
Most of the musicians were already aware of Lord Buckley,
either through personal experience or reputation, and all of
them were pleased to work with a performer who understood
where they were coming from, and who made them laugh.

Another, less-successful venture originated with his
appearance in *'Holiday In Paris.'* Just as that lower East side
production was coming to the end of its run, a relative of the
stage manager suggested he might be able to use his
connections with Ted Lewis to get His Lordship a job doing
the hip routines. Since Reno, where Lewis was appearing, was
one of Buckley's strongest locales (he'd played the *Riverside*
and been held over for three weeks), the prospects seemed
ideal. And any gig doing the hip material was automatically
considered. Excited, happy, eager to debut his new work in a
receptive atmosphere, Buckley packed up and journeyed out
to Nevada for the appearance. When he learned soon after
his arrival that the hip material was no longer to be included,
he was devastated.

The benefit at the Lexington drug center helped bring
him back to top spirits, and the birth on October 19 of his
son Richard completed the recovery. His manager, George
Greif, suggested that His Highness try the Western U.S.,
particularly Las Vegas, and Buckley – satisfied with his

success in New York but impatient to premiere the hip act as a regular feature – began to think about following the sun.

But the Royal Court was not yet quite finished with its New York meeting. At Thanksgiving the Buckleys hosted two dozen friends to a magnificent meal, including performers in all areas of showbiz. One of the performers, Anita O'Day, had known Buckley ever since the late Thirties when he helped her break into the business. During the meal, presided over by a beaming Buckley, O'Day treated the group to a series of spontaneous songs, and others joined in with bits of their own. It was a smorgasbord of talent, and Buckley contributed more than his share as well as oversaw the programming of the event.

Buckley was 44, becoming somewhat more sedate, more reflective, molding his many youthful experiences into a constantly-evolving philosophy of His world, the outside world, and beyond. The two children, a successful marriage, a relatively stable living environment – all contributed to the new insights, and were reflected in his changing outlook as a performer. Religious tales, always a vital part of his thoughts, were increasingly incorporated into his translations, as were the masterpieces of literary greats from throughout history. Both elements contained an essence that Buckley had long sought to express, each presenting truths *in great beauty and understanding.*

Lord Buckley was more than just a performer of the old classics; he was an interpreter as well, transforming old, familiar stories with relevant themes into living, eye-opening tales. His personal stature as a creative performer was mirrored in his life. His Lordship became increasingly royal in his bearing and demeanor, and the Court prospered. However, that is not to say Buckley had suddenly changed his ways completely.

One afternoon in New York, accompanying musician Joe McDonald on a trip to Times Square, Buckley followed his friend into a hobby store where McDonald had spied an impressive – and expensive – model car. McDonald, having dug deep to purchase the car, was leaving the shop explaining the wonderful intricacies of the model, when His Highness asked to examine the *toy* and see for himself just what was so special about it. McDonald hesitated a second, but handed over his new acquisition when confronted with an expectant look from Lord Buckley – a look he knew foretold a diatribe if he resisted.

As they walked out into the throng of midday Manhattan, Buckley determined that the model must've cost so much because of its mechanics, and decided to check out his theory then and there. As the shocked McDonald looked on in horror, Buckley activated the motor and turned the car loose in the street. They both followed the erratic course of the tiny vehicle as it disappeared through the legs of pedestrians and headed into the roadway – Buckley with an impressed smile, and McDonald with a grey pallor.

"Your Lordship was correct," Buckley intoned, "It *was* a very good model."

Despite occasional respites, Buckley remained as busy as ever, if not more so. With two children to supervise, and the same hectic lifestyle for both Lord and Lady Buckley, it was somewhat of a mutual miracle when Charles Booth (later Tubby Boots/Princess Lily, a female impersonator) showed up in New York looking for a place to stay.

Tubby (for his extensive girth) had run away from home in Baltimore, where he'd watched His Lordship perform from the time he was eight years old. In fact, Buckley once brought him up onstage at the *Hippodrome*, and Tubby was so captivated he invited Lord and Lady Buckley to a public pool to meet his friends. To his great surprise and delight, they'd shown up.

Now he was in New York looking for a home, and he remembered Buckley's instructions to look him up if ever he were in town. His timing was perfect. Tubby was good with

children; the Buckleys needed a babysitter. The interface was
ideal.

Every morning Lizbeth would get up early, meet
Tubby at the front door with the kids, and set off for three
hours of dance classes. Tubby would wheel the strollers to
nearby Central Park and look after the infants while she was
gone. When Lizbeth finished her classes, she'd pick up the
kids and return to the apartment, where she'd usually find
Buckley deep in intellectual discussion with Lord Edward
Michaels, his old friend from Hollywood. They'd all go out to
lunch at Lindy's (that is, lunch for her, breakfast for them),
and the conversations would continue. Tubby supplemented
the Buckley's income with the salary he earned at the *Three
Deuces* as an emcee, and he became a temporary member of
the Royal family.

Unfortunately, the course of a Buckley – even an
honorary Buckley – did not always run smooth. "I was about
thirteen years old," Tubby explains, "and His Lordship got
me a job emceeing at the *Three Deuces* at 52nd Street (a
burlesque club) – I was the only one in the household
working regularly.

"So, one night before I went to work, I was taking a
bath in the tub, sitting there reading these New York journals,
and I'm singing 'La, la, la la' and His Lordship said 'Sing out,

Lil, it's beautiful. Let me hear those notes!' And I'm trying to make the water warmer by turning the hot water on with my foot. All of a sudden, the pressure from the boiler, which was right behind the valve, pushed it off and I was yelling 'Help! Help!' as hot, steaming water was coming at me. The harder I tried to get out of the tub, the pressure of the water would throw me down again. And I'm screaming 'Help!' and His Lordship says 'Sing out Lil, that's a beautiful note!' He thought I was rehearsing.

"Finally, he comes into the bathroom, and realizing I was going into shock, he went into one of his routines: 'God Lily, you look like a lobster, we must get some butter. Lizbeth, get some butter, Lily has burned herself. We must butter up the bitch.' And I'm saying, 'call an ambulance, call a doctor, I'm dying.' And he says, 'You've never looked so good in your life...' So they butter me up from top to bottom and wrap me in a blanket. Meanwhile, I'm telling them to get a doctor. 'Control yourself,' His Lordship says. 'If you're a little upset, stop by the emergency ward and let them put some salve on it. But make your show tonight. Showbiz must get on.' He was trying to calm me down; he knew how badly I was burned. He figured by joking with me I'd stop by the hospital and they'd take care of me. So I go to the hospital and get an intern who instead of keeping me puts salve all over me and wraps the burns.

"So here I am, wrapped up like a mummy, and I show up at the *Three Deuces*. Big blisters are building up under the bandages, and I pass out onstage. They take me in an ambulance to the hospital and I'm there for nine weeks under an oxygen tent – so the burns would heal. Every day I hear this nurse go by saying, 'My god we've got royalty here. Must be incognito.' Finally I asked her what she meant and she said, 'There's a telegram here for Prince Charles of Booth.' I read it and it says 'Dear Lil. We miss your love here at the castle. Please get well soon.'

"Well, every day His Lordship would bring me a box of chocolates. One day I turned the television on and there's His Lordship on a gameshow called *'Play Ball'* and one of the sponsors was a chocolate company and he got the candy for nothing!

"Now, after nine weeks, I'm finally ready to leave. His Lordship tells me he can't pick me up because he had the television show. But he said 'don't worry about it Lil. Go home and everything will be fine.' I show up at the desk, getting ready to check out – owing them this fantastic astronomical fee – and I don't have two cents in my pocket. I walk up to the desk and say 'Right now I'm financially embarrassed, but I'll be more than happy to try to pay it once I'm back on my feet.' And she looks at the bill and says it's paid! So I asked her who paid it, and she says 'A Lord Buckley.' Tears come to my eyes – His Lordship finally came through for me!

"I went home and there's His Lordship, and I say, 'I can't believe it: $5000 to get me out of the hospital! 'Nothing's too good for you,' he says. 'Here's a plane ticket. I want you to go down to Florida and recuperate, enjoy yourself, get back your health.' So I'm down in Florida and I get a letter from a lawyer: 'Please sign this release. We've already given your uncle the $30,000.' My uncle? $30,000? Well, His Lordship had the great nerve to go to the building owners and threaten to sue for a million dollars because 'his nephew,' who was only thirteen, had been in the hospital for nine weeks, scarred for life, ruined his career... and he talked them into a $30,000 settlement. Of which, he gave $5,000 to the hospital, a plane ticket plus the $500 to me.

"Now I call him on the phone and say: 'You sonuvabitch.' But His Lordship said, 'Lil, would you ever have thought of it? Would you have had the money for the hospital bills? The vacation? I needed money – the government's on my ass, so I came up with the idea!' I was so mad I didn't speak with him again for four years."

Actually, according to Lady Buckley, the apartment manager approached His Lordship about the settlement – which was somewhat less than $30,000 – but whatever the actual circumstances, virtually none of the money remained in Buckley's pocket when the episode was completed.

Early in 1951, Buckley called up David Verne with a cryptic but urgent-sounding message to "meet me at the Astor Hotel." Verne rushed down to the hotel and was met by a secretive Buckley, who quickly shuttled him off to a large closet where he proceeded to get his friend stoned with all haste. "What's the urgency?" Verne asked, only to have Buckley explain he had a very special show to perform in just a few minutes and he wanted David to be there.

When they left the closet and went to the large room where 2000 men in dark suits listened to a speaker address their association, Lord Buckley explained. "They're all police detectives," he said mischievously, and he went on to perform the 4-person pantomime "lightning fast and perfect." The audience of policemen loved the show, and Buckley gloried in his little un-announced surprise.

Not everyone was carefree and happy during the early Fifties, however, and much of the blame for a widespread national malaise must be laid at the feet of the junior senator from Wisconsin, Joseph McCarthy. As Chairman of the

Senate's Government Operations Committee and of its
Subcommittee on Investigations, McCarthy stunned the
country with supposed revelations about communists in the
American government.

Coming as they did at a time when the U.S. was openly
terrified about the newly-developed Russian atomic bomb,
these '*revelations*' struck home with frightening intensity.
Hearsay, rumor, and suspicion became the tools of
McCarthyism, and no one was immune from the Senator's
often-unsubstantiated but always vituperative attacks.
Entertainers, from all areas of showbusiness, were among the
citizens hardest hit outside of government. The notorious
'blacklists,' which barred certain performers suspected of
communist sympathies from working, slandered many
innocent but eccentric personalities, and ruined their careers.
Though these blacklisted persons were often treated as
pariahs in social as well as professional environments,
Buckley made it a point to visit friends and acquaintances he
knew who had been subjected to this witch-hunt and reassure
them with his presence and his humor. A short piece entitled
"The Bomb" pointedly explained his belief that humor was the
greatest weapon against fear, and in both public and private
circles he used that weapon to bring rationality and
compassion to his world.

After one such trip to visit a friend on *The List,* Buckley and David Verne emerged from the Algonquin Hotel to find it "raining cats and dogs, with no hope of getting a cab."

"Why don't we just walk home?" His Lordship suggested.

"From 44th St. to 71st?" Verne questioned with an eye to the ever-deepening puddles.

"Let's not be a shirker, man!" Buckley exclaimed, and he led the way as the two of them walked the thirty blocks at a brisk pace in the pouring rain. Arriving back at the apartment drenching wet, Buckley immediately announced he was going to change into something a bit drier.

"But what about me?" Verne asked as the water pooled around his feet.

"Well, Your Grace," Buckley said with a smile, "now I have dry clothes and you don't."

For the next six months, Buckley worked constantly in New York City clubs, earning good money but spending most of it, as was his habit. Life was pleasant, the Royal Court evolved to ever-higher plateaus, but Buckley wasn't satisfied. Although his hip material kept the Court laughing, club owners in New York just wouldn't take a chance with it. For years Buckley had fine-tuned the material, perfecting a relevant act that not only entertained but enlightened, and by 1951 he was more than ready to take it to the public.

So when his manager, George Greif, offered him a gig in California and a possible appearance in a film, it was just the potential break he had been waiting for. *California*: perhaps there his hip new world could find a home amongst the swingers of Hollywood. And besides, it would be an *adventure*, and Buckley could never say no to an adventure.

On June 26th, Lord Buckley boarded a plane for Los Angeles, and with his departure the era of the Grand New York Royal Court came to an end.

CHAPTER 7

Los Angeles in the early fifties was a town exploding with excitement, anticipation, and big dreams. The movie industry flourished with established stars such as Gable, Bogart, Hepburn, and Garson, and newcomers like James Dean and Marilyn Monroe. Television began to move westward out of New York, where such contemporaries of Buckley as Milton Berle and Red Skelton had carved out a new audience and a new prestige. It was clearly the *in* place, a land of opportunity.

After touching base with Greif in L.A., Buckley traveled to Palm Springs where he met with the producer of a Twentieth Century Fox film titled, *We're Not Married*, starring Fred Allen, Ginger Rogers, and a very young Marilyn Monroe. The two men hit it off immediately, and His Lordship was signed to appear in a short segment. After completing the deal, Buckley went back to the L.A. area and found a house to rent in Encino, where his family met him after coming out from New York. A gig at *Charlie Foy's* in the Valley kept him settled for a short time, but Encino was just too square for the Royal Court, and almost immediately the Buckleys moved again – first to Laurel Canyon and then to the far outskirts of Los Angeles influence, Malibu Lake. In the quiet, country setting of the lake, Lord Buckley removed himself from the Hollywood environment that attracted him as a performer, but repelled him as a father and enlightened individual.

Because he had to spend some time in that environment to film his part, he tolerated the surroundings for the advancement of his career and the good times that ensued. As friends had worried, Lord Buckley was not the easiest actor to work with. He arrived late, joked with everyone on the set, and generally disrupted filming as he always disrupted everything wherever he went. But by the conclusion of the movie, a friend who wandered in to see how he was doing was only partially surprised to see Buckley surrounded by a captivated group of fellow actors and technicians, listening to his stories between set-ups.

The part was short and not overly challenging (Buckley played a harried radio director attempting to handle Allen and Rogers), but it promised to open the door for more satisfying roles in the future. Sadly, that was not to be the case. The film was not particularly successful and Buckley's role gave him little room to shine.

But in other media Buckley was making a move, most notably with RCA Records. Jack Lewis had met His Lordship in N.Y., and was so convinced of his considerable potential that he arranged a recording session with Lord Buckley backed by a jazz orchestra. They recorded the album twice – the first time Buckley apparently had difficulty with his false teeth and was unintelligible. When it was finally finished, Lewis played the recording for a committee of RCA execs. They weren't quite sure what it was, but they agreed it was something unique and special. Jack wrote the album notes, but it was three years before the material was released.

Returning to Las Vegas, which was rapidly becoming one of his favorite locales, Lord Buckley played the El Rancho in 1951 and won a whole new coterie of fans. One, Betty Koons, remembers, "We sat there all afternoon listening to him. At first, we couldn't quite make out everything he was saying, but after a while we got used to the pattern and loved it." Buckley made himself highly visible about town, often wearing purple shorts and an orange jacket as he strolled through the plush hotels. His performances earned him not only raves but two more bookings the next year, and he brought the news back to L.A. with even greater appreciation for Vegas.

Aside from his professional interests, Lord Buckley was keenly interested in the youth of America, and felt that his hip monologues in particular were as well-suited to young people as their parents. Working with an old friend, Harry Seybold, who at the time was radio's *'Raven'* at KGFJ in the San Fernando area, Buckley did assemblies at local high schools with such early rock & roll groups as *The Platters*. Though the rock & rollers were considered strange and far-out, Buckley usually succeeded in completely overshadowing their accomplishments. Of course, he was perhaps a bit more hip, and often a good deal more electrifying.

"You're all masturbating!" he'd announce loudly as soon as he took the stage, and even those teens who didn't know what he was talking about knew from their friends' reactions that the distinguished man onstage had earned their attention. With all eyes staring in anxious anticipation, Buckley would proceed to perform *The Nazz* or another hip translation just as he'd present them to an older group, and receive audience response at least as great as from his peers. The children accepted the beauty of the tone, cadence, and drama of the works, even if they couldn't understand specific words. And when he advised them to read all they could and practice graciousness, they listened as their teachers nodded in agreement.

Of course, Buckley was not always quite so gracious himself. At a gig in Tahoe, he got horribly drunk on the first night and was fired, and after playing a show with Frank Sinatra in Hawaii, he marched sixteen people totally nude through the lobby of the Royal Hawaiian Hotel. Nonetheless, his periods of rambunctious insanity seemed to be giving way to an ever-expanding consciousness, and though nearly every out-of-town booking required him to play the old standard material, in-town acceptance of his hip act was growing. Gigs still came frequently, but the old days of big salaries and unlimited expenditures were rapidly coming to an end.

Playing a date in Toledo, Ohio with Ella Fitzgerald, Lord Buckley found himself in a situation where his hip emceeing and monologues flew over the heads of most in his audience. The club was owned by an Asian gentleman, whose comprehension of Buckley's rapid-fire, hip jargon-studded lingo matched that of his audiences; it wasn't long before he decided that Lord Buckley might be better suited elsewhere and he offered to pay off the remainder of the contract.   His Lordship refused the offer in no uncertain terms, and a war of nerves ensued.

For two days the owner frowned at Buckley, and muttered, and renewed his offer to send him on his way. For two days His Lordship ignored his employer and continued to aim his business at an audience that for the most part didn't know what the hell he was talking about. Finally, the owner's patience wore out and he made the mistake of walking onstage while Buckley was performing, to purposely distract and anger him.

With biting indignation, Buckley threw off his jacket, nearly tore off his shirt, and tossed it to the owner.

"Bring it back in two days. No starch," His Lordship ordered, and the audience exploded. In that one moment of transformation the audience found its key to Buckley's world, and they and their friends packed the room for the remainder of the three-week gig.

Moving on to St. Louis, His Lordship found himself stranded without sufficient funds to fly home. Calling upon his friend Ted Travers to intercede with their mutual friend Frank Sinatra, who was also in town, Buckley promised to use any money provided for travelling, not partying. Sinatra came through, and had His Lordship driven to the airport. But when Frank returned to play his next show, who did he find at ringside? Lord Buckley was put on the next plane west.

Playing a gig at the *Orpheum* in San Francisco, His Lordship introduced his sisters, Nell and Mabel, to a taste of the worldly entertainment life. "This was between shows," Nell recalls. "Dick told Mabel that we had time 'for a nice, cool ice cream soda,' so he took her arm, and I took the arm of Nat King Cole, who was backstage with Dick, and here we are marching up the street – it made Mabel terribly upset that I was walking with a black man.

"But Dick cooled her down – told her what a wonderful man he was and 'shame on her and where was her religion?' He did it in a nice way, you know.

"Well, we came to a bar, and Dick told her it was an ice cream parlor because she'd've died if she knew it was a bar, and when we walked in Dick gave the bartender some sort of sign so when Mabel climbed up on the crushed velvet stools and ordered an ice cream soda they sent out for it and brought it to her. She just raved about that place, said it was the most beautiful ice cream parlor she'd ever been in."

Appearances in Vegas, at the *El Rancho*, and in Reno, at the *Riverside* and *Harold's*, continued to provide both needed money and – even more essential – new audiences. A September 1951 show at the El Rancho earned a strong *VARIETY* review:

"Dick Buckley is possibly the surprise comedy turn of the year. He delivers patter in pompous British lingo, surprises by uncanny impresh of Louis Armstrong, then ropes roars with audience participation gimmick, bringing three males, one femme onstage. Has foils mouth silently while he does all voices of funny Amos 'n Andy sketch. Breaks the whole place up."

In April, Buckley was back at the *El Rancho* on a bill that included Samia Gamal and Tony Bennett. In May, he was off to Reno again for the opening of the new *Golden Theater Restaurant*, appearing there with old friends Cab Calloway and Polly Bergen. Several gigs at *Charlie Foy's* made him almost a regular, and his Amos and Andy act – seen by millions during appearances on Ed Sullivan's show – still brought laughter and cheers.

During one engagement at *Foy's*, Ed "Prince Eaglehead" Randolph learned the hard way that Lord Buckley could spin a tale to his own ends at the spur of the moment – or the spur of desire. Buckley convinced Eaglehead he desperately needed money to buy new tires, and managed to wheedle $50 out of the less-than-flush vending machine salesman. When Eaglehead next saw His Highness, he noticed the tires were still worn, and asked what he had done with the money.

Lord Buckley explained he'd spent it on *grass*. But rather than apologize for his action, he chastised Randolph for allowing it to happen. "It's your fault, Eaglehead," he explained crossly, "for putting temptation in front of me."

Temptation never seemed to leave His Lordship alone for long, although he was usually able to overcome, or at least ameliorate its effects through talent, personality, and perseverance. Sometimes his efforts were just too much for the *average Joe* to appreciate, as when he was asked to audition at MGM studios for a group of production personnel who were considering him for film roles. His friend Stewart Whitman, an actor who'd met Buckley through George Greif, suggested to the MGM people that His Lordship's incredible charisma and diverse talents would be ideal for films, and so the meeting was arranged.

No sooner had Lord Buckley been introduced to the studio people, than he launched into a series of 35 characterizations, one after another, so real, so zany, and so different, that he frightened the filmmakers. They had already heard of his reputation for being uncontrollable, and now his demonstration of acting ability was so overwhelming they feared he was insane. So once again His Lordship missed the one 'big chance' that could have set him up for the *big time*. Not too surprisingly, although he was upset at their reaction, he was very pleased his characters were so believable.

As the year came to a close, Buckley journeyed to Bakersfield for a gig, where his sister Nell took the opportunity to meet with her much-travelled, little-seen brother. Having much to catch up with, the two siblings shared the same room and stayed up all night discussing their recent pasts. Just as morning was breaking, a shudder passed through the building – earthquake! Buckley was up instantly and roaring directions to everyone within earshot. "Out of the building!" he insisted forcefully, but without a trace of panic. "Out here, out by the pool!"

Once he had assembled the majority of the guests at poolside, he kept them from returning to the building until all after-shocks were gone by improvising a little show to entertain them. With great pomp and circumstance, Lord Buckley announced he was about to demonstrate a feat accomplished only once before in the history of mankind: he was going to walk across the pool. Already shaken by the quake, his audience didn't know whether to laugh or flee from this seemingly serious gentleman. Buckley quickly decided the question for them.

Edging tentatively to the lip of the pool, Buckley feigned meditation and stepped bravely off the side. He sank without a word. But when he surfaced, the people were laughing and he was too. He pulled himself out of the water to appreciative applause, and announced, "Now I will continue." A few more bits kept their attention until the all-clear was given.

Buckley returned to Malibu Lake for a short while, and then set out again on the road. By this time, he and Lizbeth had decided that the Lake, though beautiful, was too far removed from the action Buckley sought when he moved to the Coast, and Lizbeth pledged to look for a new home while His Lordship was gone.

At a real estate office, Lizbeth ran into an elderly woman who was attempting to rent-out a house at 6672 Whitley Terrace in

Northeast Hollywood. One look at the place, and Lady B. knew she had to have it. A large, impressive house that resembled a modern urban castle, the Whitley Terrace Palace was the perfect setting for Buckley and the Royal Court. Lizbeth convinced the owner – later dubbed 'The Witch' by Buckley – to lower the rent and allow her to move in at once. Calling upon Stewart Whitman and other Buckley friends, the Buckleys were moved into their new home in no time.

Immediately, Lady B. began preparing the Castle for the return of His Lordship. A week later – returned from the road – Lord Buckley was aglow with satisfaction as Lizbeth ushered him into his new home. With a large ballroom, beautifully- prepared hardwood floors, a grand piano, and both a quiet, expensive neighborhood and an invigorating view, Buckley was truly *home* at last. All his dreams for the Royal Court had centered on such a fitting locale, and now

that it was his, the Court flourished as never before. The
Hollywood Castle became a rallying point for every hip
entertainer on the Coast: Stan Getz, Benny Carter, Duke
Ellington, Count Basie, Dana Andrews, Scott Brady, Huntz
Hall, Larry Storch, and many, many others were frequent
house guests. The rich, the poor, the famous, and the
unknown – they all participated in the fun and mind
expansion that was the Whitley Royal Court.

"His life was so much better and powerful than
everybody else's," Charles Tacot recalls. "He didn't want to
go to theirs, so they either came to his life or forget it. If he
didn't have $25 in his pocket, he'd borrow $100 to buy pork
chops to feed 95 bimbos, and three bottles of champagne to
wash it down. There were stars in Hollywood making a
million dollars who didn't have the fun he did. He came to
realize that many people who had all those things were
fucking miserable, and that the party was the answer – it went
on every night, rain or shine. He had more fun than anyone,
every goddamn day. But after he'd get all these people all
jacked up, suddenly he'd be gone. And they'd all drop back to
what they were in life – which was very little compared to
what they were when he was there."

And yet, as fine as life seemed at Whitley Terrace, the
move to Hollywood marked a sudden lull in His Lordship's

career, a lull so severe that Buckley soon became notorious among his friends for his wide variety of borrowing tactics. Sometimes he would pawn or sell something he owned – actor/director Gene Nelson bought cufflinks and a watch from His Lordship, but balked at buying a vacuum cleaner. At other times, he would cajole, hint, even demand the payment of money, as if his years of generosity and Royal peerage entitled him to a living stipend when his act wasn't clicking.

In New York, staying at the *Chesterfield Hotel* while awaiting an appearance on the Ed Sullivan show, Buckley called on his friend Richard *'Prince Owlhead'* Zalud for a loan. "He ordered me to come down with $50," Owlhead explained, "but we just didn't have it. We were going up to work the Catskills and we needed every penny. Well, he laid a rap on me about 'the fires of hell being too good for a bastard like you,' and I got pissed off and hung up. But after we got up there and were situated, I wired him the $50.

"The same day I called him up to let him know the money was on the way. His reaction? 'Ah hah! Conscience!' he roared. It broke me up."

Not that Buckley wasn't offered gigs. The creator of the cartoon *Mr. Magoo* arranged for His Lordship to audition for a job doing cartoon voiceovers, but at the initial meeting Lord Buckley pulled out a joint and lit up in clear view of the dismayed producers. As might be expected, he didn't get the job. Similar circumstances, combined with his 'difficult' reputation, made it nearly impossible to land the sort of jobs befitting His Highness. On one occasion, a booking agent walking down Sunset Blvd saw Lord Buckley coming from the other direction and none-too-subtly crossed the street. Not to be outdone, Buckley crossed the Boulevard himself and confronted the agent. To charges that his reputation as a heavy drinker made it nearly impossible for anyone to book him into the 'nicer' clubs, Richard explained his conversion to the AA-way had made his past just old news.

"But I can't book a reformed drunk," the agent insisted.

"I'm not a reformed drunk," Buckley patiently explained. "I am an *informed* drunk, and it won't interfere with my performing." The agent was eventually convinced and managed to book a date, but he was the exception. Eventually, Buckley was forced to take a job as emcee at the seedy *Strip City* club; as a family man, he needed the money. But, as Lizbeth remembers, "it really hurt him to have to go back to the sewers after 25 years."

Although working a *sewer* gnawed at his pride and professional self-esteem, Buckley maintained a cheerful exterior that continued to bring laughter into the lives of

everyone who knew him. "Every day was Christmas, and
every night was New Year's" Lizbeth recalled, as the Royal
Court swung to a higher beat.

It took money to maintain that beat, however, and His
Lordship took steps to ensure that some income was
forthcoming. As Prince Booth – Tubby Boots – remembers:
"I was working at a club in Peoria, Illinois. I had my own
radio show, and I was making $750 a week. And someone
passing through Peoria happened to mention that his
Lordship was out in California. I figured, 'let's bury the
hatchet. I'll call His Lordship.' So I picked up the phone and
called California: 'Lil, my dear girl, I know you still hate me
for what I did, but you must give me the chance to make it up
to you," His Lordship said. 'I am now in Hollywood living in
the lap of luxury, making movies, living in the Hollywood
Hills in Barbara LaMar's house. You must get on a plane and
come out here immediately, live in luxury, go into movies, do
the things you should have done already. I'll make it up to
you.'

"So here I am, giving up a $750/week job and flying to
L.A. So I thought, 'His Lordship does things in a big way,
he'll probably have a band waiting for me. Something great.'
As I get off the plane, here's Lizbeth waiting with a young
black boy and both of them have paint all over them. 'C'mon
Prince, His Lordship is in the castle waiting,' she says. So we

get in the little car, and drive up to the Hollywood Hills, and
as I walk in the door His Lordship is on the phone talking to
an agent. He said: 'I've got the greatest act for you in the
whole world: Tubby Boots. He sings, dances, everything.
Opens tonight, a hundred and a half?' He sold me for
$150/week to open that night at the *Zambra Café!*

"So I said, 'Your Lordship, I just gave up a $750 job to
come out here so you could sell me for $150? Why didn't you
just tell me you needed money? I could have kept my job and
sent you the money.' He said, 'Lil, would you have come if I
told you? If I had told you, you would have hung up!' I went
to work that night and worked every night for eight months.
Every week I gave the $150 to His Lordship.

"One week I had to clean the house, cook for all the
fucking bum actors he had living there, and give him my
whole salary. Then one day I asked him for a dollar to go to
the movies and he said to me, 'How ungrateful you can be!'
So that night I packed up and snuck out of the Castle. I heard
on the streets he called me a traitor for sneaking out. And till
the day he died, he thought I'd done something wrong. That
I'd besmudged him. But you know, I loved His Lordship like
he was my own father. He always gave me more than he
took. He showed me how to live, how to enjoy life."

Back at the Castle, Lord Buckley continued as best he could. Ensconced in his ever-present high-backed throne chair, he oversaw the festivities and provided most of the impetus. Aside from his stories, impressions, and songs, it was not unusual for His Lordship to pull out the large flat sword he kept near the throne and perform a ritualistic knighting a´ la King Arthur.

Deserving candidates would kneel at his feet and be dubbed "Prince," "Lord," "Duke," or, more rarely, "King." Women received corresponding titles. One night he decided to knight twenty-two strangers, and they were so confused and honored they let him do it.

Newly-titled royalty were expected to make a contribution to the entertainment of the Court, and impromptu songs or other bits were always part of the show. And, as Robert Mitchum relates, the Court activities didn't stop there.

"Buckley had people sitting under chairs, as though they were in a cage. If they performed well, they were rewarded with a drink. Other people would pretend to be wild animals and dart in and out biting people on the legs."

And yet, if a member of the Court did not live up to expectations, his title could also be revoked. Clyde Jones, of the Jones Brothers, was once suspected by His Lordship of making a questionable pass at Lady B, and Clyde received a telegram advising him: "Henceforth, the title Lord Jones has officially become Clyde Jones, status quo, until further notice, etc."

Woody Herman and Count Basie both played the Court, and Lord Buckley performed his recently-composed *'Pied Piper'* translation backed by Lionel Hampton. It was a time of wonder and magic.

Perhaps the high point for the Whitley Court came on New Year's Day, 1954. A huge crowd of friends, including a sizeable contingent of celebrities, gathered at the castle to ring out the old year and cheer in the new. For Buckley, the change was most welcome, as his optimistic nature anticipated better days ahead.

The house was in top form for the celebration, but, as the *Earl of Eldon* points out, the facade extended only as far as the designated party area.

"Everything looked posh and great, until we opened the kids' bedroom door and saw that it was all makeshift. But back in the main room everything was just right – waxed floors and all that. Lord Buckley came out in tux and tails and did some Louis Armstrong at the baby grand, and then he got into this monologue about everyone there being wonderful people except for 'one pompous ass.' And he looked right at me. He kept at it, over and over, until I got mad and went after him. Well, he talked me out of it, and we later sat around drinking coffee while Buckley told a story about pigeons talking to each other as they *bombed* people below. And before I left, we were good friends again."

In addition to Buckley, several others performed that night, but the audience didn't applaud. Part of the agreement for renting the house included a stipulation that noise be kept to a minimum, so instead of clapping, the Court expressed its appreciation in the form of appreciative vibrations and murmured congratulations.

There were many parties at the Castle, some larger, some more intimate. At one in early '54, in the wee hours of the morning just before breakfast, as Buckley, Mel Welles and others sat around talking, Rick Llewelyn brought up a concept that was to have a major impact on the Court.

"For years Rick Llewelyn used to talk about how people wanted him to become an evangelist," Welles remembers, "because with the success of people like Oral Roberts and others like that there were religious promoters out looking for enigmatic and dynamic people to set them up as a Billy Graham or a this or that. And Rick was approached. Well. this night, when everybody had left and there were a few diehards smoking that last joint before departing, we said that Dick should start his own religion. And out of the blue he said yes, and came up with the title *Church of the Living*

Swing, America's first jazz church, and the whole thing was a gas." Though it would take another year to realize their plans, it was a beginning.

Welles, a doctor of psychology by education, became a somewhat unique character in the Buckley Court – the Royal confidant. "I enjoyed a very special relationship with Dick Buckley, in that I was his unofficial psychologist. And where he was *on* most of the time, I enjoyed many, many hours with him where he would let it all drop off and he exposed some of his worry and discontent. So, we had a kind of different relationship than most everybody else who was enjoying the frivolities and the gay life that he created around him all the time. You know, with all the bizarre characters.

"It didn't inhibit or prohibit me from also enjoying that part of his particular private world of madness but it gave us a reason to be together at times when he had no reason to be together with anybody, and as you know he was rarely alone. One of the great things about those days was when he would go to the bathroom to languish in the tub. There would be twenty people there in the bathroom with him, sitting around on the tub and toilet and everything. Even in the bathroom, no one ever let him alone.

"A lot of people, you'd ask them, 'what was your relationship to Lord Buckley,' they'd have to admit there was

no relationship, they just showed up because there were a lot
of broads around. If you were a centrally self-indulgent
person you would show up at his place thinking maybe he'd
conduct an orgy, or something like that, because he would
conduct anything just to show people the power they had and
the power *he* had: the ability to direct and create some kind of
scene.

"Most people went for the action, because you had
musicians and singers and liberated people in a day when
there wasn't so much liberation around, and you could talk
freely. There was no prejudice against blacks, homosexuals,
or anybody. It was a positive structured environment, which
today (1978) you'll pay $1500 a month to get. It was kind of
an early Gestalt therapy session, that's what it really was.
People could go there and leave their cares and depravity for
one night and feel that they had been touched by some kind
of cross between Svengali and the Marquis de Sade – when in
reality all he was was a great entertainer and a sweet guy with
a tremendous philosophy and a tremendous love for people.
That's the heart of it, he just loved people.

"And he had a great understanding of the Black
experience – at least for a white guy – and blacks were
fascinated by him. Also, if you were just an ordinary hustler
within the framework of the entertainment world, you didn't

get invited to many heavyweight parties. You know, nobody invited you over to Robert Redford's place, or what have you.

"Even though there weren't often great film celebrities at Buckley's, there were a lot of musical celebrities. Like, you would run into a giant on the jazz scene, for example. Or you would run into singers and dancers, writers, comedians, ventriloquists, fashion designers, and all people budding in their careers. Some of them had made it, so you felt you were at a party full of luminaries of one sort or another, a really colorful experience."

Welles was one of several at the time who were convinced that His Lordship's greatest career potential lay in legit theater productions of his hip material. "If we could have put him in concert adventure theater form and surrounded him with all the proper dynamics and elements of the Jazz Age, he would have become a full winner in his lifetime." Even after a disastrous guest appearance at the *Sherman Hotel* in Chicago, both Buckley and his supporters were convinced of the viability of the medium. All that was lacking was the proper production... and a bit of education for his audiences.

"For the most part," Welles explains, "that material died because people didn't know what he was talking about. To begin with, *hip talk* was not very widespread. Frank

Sinatra, Steve Allen, and a few other people began on their television shows to use all those expressions which eventually made it so that everybody could understand hip, but at that particular time almost nobody dug it."

Added to the equation were the intricacies of Buckley himself. At 47 years old, with nearly 30 years of showbusiness behind him, His Highness was a difficult man to get to know. "You know, Buckley was a great paradox," Welles continues. "The things he did in life were very winning things. But whenever something good was about to happen, he would disappear or screw off somewhere. Something would happen to louse it up.

His relationship to the commercial entertainment world was as paradoxical in nature as he was. He wanted to make it commercially, but seemed to do things intentionally to prevent himself from making it."

At home, Buckley was a stern disciplinarian with his children, and consequently Laurie and Richard were often described as "perfect little kids." They had grown up on the road and in the company of adults, and were precocious as well as properly mannered. Buckley was not around as much as they might have hoped, but when he was, they were seldom left behind or excluded from the activities of the day – or night. "Dress the props," he'd order Lizbeth when he wanted to take them out, and they were always dressed as elegantly as their parents – when money permitted. For the children, Whitley was their own very special world, and at times their youthful zest frightened visitors. One guest, seeing Richard and Laurie running down a roped walkway to the 'pagoda' behind the house, was worried they might hurt themselves. "Don't worry," Buckley reassured him with a nearly imperceptible smile, "they are heavily insured."

Buckley created a real fantasy world for his family, and they believed in his creation so thoroughly that they lived it without question. His relationship with his first son, Fred, was something else again, however. Having seen his real father infrequently, at intervals of 2-3 years at a time, Fred knew only that Lord Buckley was an interesting character who sometimes brought him presents during unexpected and short-lived visits. It wasn't until he was 14 that a friend revealed to him Buckley was his father, and by the time the two next met, Fred was already a young man.

Buckley was constantly busy with a variety of projects, not the least of which was ridding himself of the need for booze. Though still tempted from time to time by the lure of alcohol, Lord Buckley strove to limit his consumption to moderate levels and convince his friends to do the same. Robert Mitchum was one of many who witnessed Buckley's lectures on self-destruction.

"It was like a religion to him. He'd describe drinking as ruining a temple of God and cite himself as a prime example. He'd point out a vein on his nose and use it as 'an example of the folly of strong drink.' Like a preacher, he'd hammer on the point with an inspired roar. Yet at the same time, he admitted to being *'a master of self-deception.'*"

Friends from Edward G. Robinson, Jr. to composer Mel Henke all were subjected to Buckley's fervent appeals, and in several instances the approach worked. Buckley convinced Henke to attend an AA meeting with him, and although His Lordship failed to show, Mel was helped considerably.

Despite the addition of a family and an improved home atmosphere, His Lordship was still an adventurer at heart, and was always available for an impromptu expedition. One such journey, prompted by the appearance of an old friend, Luther, who had just been released from prison, took Owlhead, Luther, Buckley, and the Whitley Witch to Las Vegas. With a brand-new car to celebrate getting out of confinement for a violation of the Mann Act – transporting a minor across state lines – Luther was ready for fun. Buckley persuaded his landlady, the Witch, to come with them, and with virtually no preparation they set off for Nevada. When they came to the state line, however, Luther insisted that *Lady Curl* get out of the car and walk across the boundary – just to be sure. No arguments could dissuade him, so as he drove slowly ahead, the old woman walked into Nevada and then got back into the car for the remainder of the trip.

Back in L.A., although bookings remained scarce and money was becoming extremely tight, His Lordship was unwilling to abandon either his lifestyle or his philosophies. In fact, after a performance at the *Sarturis Theater*, Lord Buckley took 10% of the gate – which he could have desperately used – and brought it to the local police station to contribute to the Policeman's Fund. It was his way of showing appreciation for the good work the police accomplished (and making himself known as a friend of the cops.)

Somewhat taken aback by his contribution, one officer determined that he must be either drunk or insane and threatened to jail His Highness. Buckley managed to dissuade him.

Such benevolence strained limited resources to the limit, and beyond, and by mid-1954 it became obvious that Whitley Terrace was more of a burden than could be managed. Not that Buckley didn't try his damnedest to hang on to his beloved Castle. Piece by piece, he sold most of the furniture in the house, according to Tubby Boots, until the

owner (of both house and furniture), Lady Curl, began to
notice something was amiss.

After several put-offs at which His Lordship suggested
the furniture was out being cleaned or reupholstered, a new
tact was required. When Lady Curl came to the door for her
rent, Buckley called an impromptu *Swing For Life*
ballet/exercise class in which everyone present dressed in
ballet togs and assembled in the main room — which, of
course, had been 'cleared of furniture' for the endeavor. Lady
Curl was persuaded to join-in, some chive-enlivened leftovers
were served for sustenance, and two hours later the
befuddled Whitley Witch was on her way, without the rent
and unaware the furniture was missing. But eventually, even
His Lordship couldn't hide the reality of the situation. And
so, once more the Royal Court sought a new home.
There was perhaps no less-likely spot for the Court's next site
than the house located at 22052 Hyperion, and so, not

surprisingly, the Buckley's moved in. A tiny guest house
located on a hill above a larger home, the new house was
really little more than three tiny rooms and an adjacent patio.
Reached by dozens of stairs, the house was nearly hidden
from the street and inaccessible to all except those who truly
wanted to visit. Buckley dubbed the tiny structure *'The
Crackerbox Palace,'* and the Court was in residence.

Though the bulk of the furniture consisted of six children's chairs circled around a small table, many members of the Court braved the seemingly endless stairs and the minor inconvenience to visit. Guests would take pot lunch if they dropped in unexpectedly, and more than once beans were the main course of fare. But then, as one visitor remarked, "Buckley could make a bean dinner seem like a six-course feast."

One of the more distinguished guests at the Palace was actress Greer Garson, who stopped by to visit with Lord and Lady Buckley and graciously accepted her surroundings without notice.

Professionally, Lord Buckley was scuffling. He was still hot in Vegas, playing the *Golden Nugget* in August of '54, and in Reno, but local gigs were scarce. One bright note was an album he recorded on a portable Ampex recorder at Mel Welles' home, with Charles Tacot the engineer. Released on the *VAYA* label, the LP contained such classics as *"Nero"* and *"Lion's Breath,"* and became one of the first widely-circulated comedy LP recordings. Dana Andrews was so impressed by the album that he invited the Buckleys to his home. An impromptu performance developed – as it did so often whenever His Lordship was around – and Andrews' front lawn became the site of Buckley's skits and monologues as well as the children's presentation of *'Baa Baa Black Sheep.'*

In Reno, His Lordship was regarded by friends as visiting royalty. On one tour to northern Nevada, the family piled into the Ferryland Express – a fire-red English Ford with lift-up windshield and an American flag waving from the antenna – and with a second car drove caravan-style to an engagement at the *Mapes* with Helen Tribbell. As Tacot remembers: "We stayed at this spa/motel, a resort with little individual cabins. Each cabin had a tiled hot tub with mineral water piped in.

"There was a woman in Reno who ran a whorehouse, and they'd close-up when Dick came to town, in his honor. They sent all the girls away, and we'd have the main house all to ourselves. She'd cook chicken and dumplings – it was her specialty – and they had all this booze, and the party went on every night after the show for the week he was in town. It was great. They loved Buckley."

Such lavished appreciation was largely personal, however, as managers and club owners still tried to figure out what Buckley was all about. One person who understood His Lordship was novelist Henry Miller, who sent Lord Buckley the following letter, dated Feb. 15, 1955:

"Dear Lord Buckley:

"A man in Reseda, California made me a gift of the album *"Euphoria"* some weeks ago. Since then, my wife and I have played the recording over numerous times, and when the right friend comes along, we force him to sit down and listen to it. Particularly the selection called *'The Nazz,'* which I consider a classic and, at the same time, like nothing I have ever heard before in any language. For weeks now we have been unable to advise our friends where to obtain the record, no address being given on the recording, which I think is a grave omission – for you and all concerned. Only by great good luck did I get on to the track, through writing the music critic of the *San Francisco Chronicle.* In the interim, I had written numerous people I thought ought to know you and your recording. How a man with your gift can remain 'unknown' to so many people is still a mystery to me. I should have thought that by this time you would be as well-known as say, Charles Laughton.

"If the *Vaya* people, or the distributors, have any literature about you which I might have to distribute among my friends here and abroad, I would thank you to let me know. You may well be able to do without the publicity, but I doubt that my friends can do without you. What you have is unique. If you had access to the pulpit, you would undoubtedly make 'converts' by the millions. I say it as a writer who knows the power of language, the miracles it can work. I somehow assume that you also composed the scripts you so magnificently render. But whether you did or not makes no difference. You and you alone created them, made them live and thereby made us who listen live a little more.

"What I would love to know, my dear Lord Buckley, is – have you made any other recordings? And if not, why not? It seems to me that you have a world to conquer. You haven't a single rival that I can think of. Even 'straight' renderings from the Bible, from Shakespeare, from Lautreamont, from Rimbaud, would startle the frogs, the snails, the turtles who sit and listen to television night after night. I spoke of *"The Nazz"* above, but the *"Murder"* piece is almost equally effective. I believe you could even take a passage from *"The Stones of Venice"* (o shades of Ruskin!) and make us sway and froth at the mouth.

"I stop lest you think I have lost all sense of judgement. Read between the lines, if you will, and know that my enthusiasm and sincerity are genuine. May these few words give you the courage to continue unabashed. And, if ever you should be passing this way, be assured of a hearty welcome here.

Sincerely yours,

Henry Miller"

Such words of praise heartened Lord Buckley, and helped him overcome the sorrow of the loss of his mother at age 90. The overwhelming reassurance of a man such as Miller, who His Lordship respected so highly, helped compensate for his temporary lack of public support, yet made his predicament all the more ironic.

Buckley's in-town gigs were still infrequent and inadequate, including a stint at the 'Near 'n Far' strip joint on Sunset Blvd. Money was nearly non-existent, but Buckley had the heart to keep on scuffling. An episode at the *Los Paritos* Mexican restaurant illustrated the degree of his difficulties, as well as his ever-present goodwill towards others. He and Cecil Rogis had finished eating and were about to leave, when Lord Buckley excused himself for a second and strolled casually down the aisle past the booths, taking buns and tortillas and stuffing them into his pockets. "Hard times are afoot," he explained to Rogis. But when the waitress confronted him and wondered why such a dignified looking gentleman was collecting leftovers, he said "I'm on social security – my number is 1." Actually, His Lordship frequently kept food in his pockets during those difficult times, so that when he went to parties, he had something to offer his friends.

The parties were still a regular occurrence, but the fare was noticeably simpler and the number of visitors to the Court a good deal smaller. Buckley managed to attend other celebrations, however, including one rather boisterous get-together up in Verduga Canyon. Several hours of all-out partying had exhausted the supply of beer, and one of the party-goers was sent out to resupply the group. Unfortunately, while backing down a steep hill he hit a restraining wall, and the owners of the house called the police.

When the officers arrived at the house where the party was being held, Buckley answered the door wearing just undershorts, a t-shirt, socks, and supporters. When the police asked him if there was a party going on, Lord Buckley looked surprised. "A party? Here?" His Highness asked innocently. "No, no, it must be next door." Somewhat dubious, but unwilling to challenge such a respectable-seeming fellow, they left.

Despite all the setbacks, Buckley's sense of humor remained strong, though it frequently took on a sharp edge due to his economic situation. At the Villas Viscotti, meeting friends for lunch, Buckley showed up with a gas nozzle from a service station pump. Without a word, he put it down in the middle of the table and looked to his friends for a reaction. He got it. "What the hell is that for?" one buddy asked. Buckley smiled with a look of complete satisfaction. "I acquired this for just $5, and it must be worth at least $10. This is how I make my living. *Investments* are the name of the game."

Actually, trying to make the hip act go was the name of the game, and in May 1955 Buckley got another shot in the arm when *Limb* magazine, one of the first jazz-oriented mags in the country, decided to print his *Julius Caesar* piece. There's little doubt that when the magazine's small, select audience read *"Hipsters, Flipsters, and Finger-Popping Daddies, Knock me your lobes,"* they knew something original and hot was on the scene. But His Lordship's expectations were not immediately borne out, for though the article helped cement his reputation among those who already knew him, and extend it to those of the same mind who were lucky enough to see the magazine, it did little to extend his fame to the vast 'Eisenhower generation' with its preoccupation with 3-D glasses, Davy Crockett coonskin caps, and hula hoops.

It became increasingly obvious to Buckley and his friends that if His Lordship was going to break the hip material into the mainstream of American entertainment, he'd have to do it himself.

Television was dominated by the likes of Milton Berle, Phil Silvers, and Sid Caesar – great comedians, but rooted more in the 30's and 40's than in the 60's and 70's – where

Lord Buckley's consciousness was already exploring new worlds. Even his good friend Ed Sullivan, knowing his audience wasn't yet ready to accept Lord Buckley's vision of the future, insisted that Richard stick to the schtick that was expected of him.

Buckley was not about to sit idly by. So, on September 16th, Lord Buckley and select members of the Royal Court presented an after-hours production at the *Music Box Theater*, a 2 a.m. show entitled *'The House of Lords.'* Featuring Lord Buckley, the cast also included Crown Prince Stork Legs (Scott Brady), and such Court notables as Sir Cliff-Hanger, Prince Foxtails, Prince Douglas, Prince Deems, and assorted court jesters.

Onstage, behind the performers, Bob Dewitt painted a mural as the show progressed, described by one spectator as "a fat woman floating in space." Red Rodney played trumpet and Kenny Drew manned the piano as an all-star jazz group backed the series of skits, monologues, and ad-lib material witnessed by a hip, pot-smoking crowd of about 100.

With such intimate successes fueling his natural enthusiasm, a guest appearance on the Groucho Marx *'Bet Your Life'* television game show amounted to a major breakthrough. For once, the event matched His Lordship's preconceived notion, as Groucho gave Lord Buckley free reign to embellish his 'role' as a contestant into a classic piece of business. The audience roared, Groucho played it to the hilt, and Buckley was seen by millions across the nation. If only he could get such national publicity in a forum that allowed him to be himself, his own cosmic, charismatic self, THEN the Royal Court would finally get its just desserts.

But the break still wasn't there. Temporarily barred from a vast national audience, Buckley took his show to whatever audience he could find, or found him. The Earl of Eldon persuaded him to travel to L.A. City College, to promote His Lordship and to see what effect he would have on the city's youth. They arrived at the campus at noon, and immediately Lord Buckley began performing. With the powerful Shakespearean voice he had developed during all his years on the stage, Buckley regaled first just a few, and then increasing numbers of students in the middle of a grassy quadrangle. Soon the area was mobbed with cheering college students, most of whom were exposed for the first time to a 'real beatnik.'

A few weeks later, the entire Buckley family piled into Eldon's Studebaker convertible and headed out to Santa Monica Beach, then one of the most swinging hang-outs on the coast. While everyone was relaxing on the beach, a ukulele appeared from somewhere and Lord Buckley was right there, ready to go. A few Hawaiian ditties led to some monologues, and when a sizeable crowd had gathered, including Peter Lorre, Eldon passed his hat "to gather grocery money, which at the time was quite scarce."

If money was scarce, an assortment of drugs was not, including marijuana, cocaine, and peyote. The Crackerbox Palace was definitely a party pad, and the alternative highs helped keep His Highness away from booze. The crowd at the Palace, and in Hollywood, was a wild, free group of California's young, talented, creative people, both men and women. Taboos, at least those invented by society, were not flaunted so much as ignored. To Lord Buckley and his Court, if it made you happy and didn't hurt anyone else, it wasn't bad.

One night, after a late show that finished around 4 a.m., Buckley, Harry Seybold, Ben Pollack, Art Laboe, Deacon Ware, and several others went out to the *Carolina Pines* restaurant for an early breakfast, and ensconced themselves in a rear booth to talk and relax. Midway through their meal, a stripper known to all strolled in and was greeted warmly by everyone, but extremely warmly by one lady in particular who was seated with them. As the woman complimented the newly-arrived stripper profusely for several minutes, it became evident where her sexual preferences lay and the men promoted the budding relationship with stoned good humor.

"Talk to each other!" Buckley suggested with snapping fingers beating an upbeat rhythm, and after several moments of rather intimate conversation it was suggested that the whole party move to Chef Herbie's restaurant, where the owner could be persuaded to re-open for their group endeavor. No sooner had they arrived at Herbie's, and situated themselves, than the two women stripped to the waist and began to make passionate love in one of the booths. Buckley and Ware led a boisterous cheering session as the women got it on; when they were finished, the group had breakfast as planned and broke up to head for home as the sun came up.

Despite Buckley's continued wild life, he remained a robust and athletic man who understood perfectly well the importance of keeping one's body in shape, even if he wasn't always able to carry out his own good intentions. As healthy as he seemed, he was keenly aware that others were not so lucky. In late '55, telethons for raising funds to help the disabled were just becoming popular, having been 'invented' by the Arthritis Foundation in New York City earlier that year. Buoyed by the success of the N.Y. show, the Foundation decided to expand the principle to Providence, Rhode Island, where WJAR was to host a similar television fund-raiser. David Martin was hired to do pre-production work for the company in charge of arranging the program, primarily to find local talent to supplement the national stars promised by the overseeing firm.

According to Martin: "The talent listed to appear read like a Who's Who of showbiz – Eddie Fisher, Dinah Shore, Polly Bergen, and many others. It looked like another big success. But then, just by accident, I happened to find out that Polly Bergen was booked for Vegas that same weekend, so I realized I'd better check up on the other bookings to see if they were firmed up or just wishful thinking. It turns out *none* of the advertised stars had actually committed to the show."

Martin suggested to his boss that the show be cancelled, but because of legal, financial, and ego problems, it was decided that the show must go on, despite the obvious potential for a complete fiasco. The show opened, ironically enough, with *"You'll Never Walk Alone,"* and the introduction of all the local and Arthritis Foundation dignitaries.

Jack Carter had been persuaded at the last minute to appear for the benefit, and he opened the program by flagrantly insulting every Italian within 50 miles. The calls poured in – all outraged. The mood backstage was bleak, as it appeared that the evening and following day would be long indeed. When singer Anita Ellis finally arrived – as a favor to her friend Dave Martin – 1200 people were packed into the auditorium, and their demands to see stars were becoming increasingly vocal and unfriendly. In addition to the crowd inside, long lines of eager spectators waited none-too-patiently outside as the hours dragged by.

Ellis had brought two of her friends with her to try to bolster the program, and though neither billed nor even expected, Joey English and Lord Buckley were ready to do anything to assist their friend and the Foundation. Neither Martin nor his boss knew who Buckley was, but with the situation approaching the critical stage, they sent him out to woo the savage throng. He did his best, mixing traditional tales, impressions, even a song or two, but the people were adamant in their desire to see the stars. By 4 a.m. everyone realized the problem was getting out of hand, and as a last gasp effort the company in charge turned the program over to David Martin, who immediately turned it over to Buckley, and a few other little-known performers.

Martin made an announcement that tactfully explained the situation, and then announced: "Your emcee for the remainder of the telethon, Lord Richard Buckley!" Some of those present had seen Buckley perform earlier, and they applauded politely, but many others had no idea who this distinguished-looking gentleman might be. Completely comfortable and in control as master of ceremonies, Buckley quickly demonstrated just who he, and the rest of the cast were, by changing the pace and structure of the program without detracting from the serious nature of the event. "He was beautiful," Martin remembers. "He did everything we asked him to do and more, and yet played it completely straight, for the most part."

Within an hour after Buckley and his friends took over, the phones began to ring, and by 5 p.m., when the show closed, the crowd was cheering for all the performers – urged on and excited by Buckley's long-practiced art of audience control. It must have seemed like deja vu for the 49-year-old Walkathon veteran: the people, the cheers, the fun. But this time it was just a one-day affair, and the once ebony black hair and moustache were showing touches of grey. Nonetheless, whereas the Foundation had raised only $3000 during the first part of the telethon, during the final twelve hours when His Lordship was at the microphone, over $28,000 was donated!

Returning to California and the Crackerbox Palace, Lord Buckley found little had changed in his short absence. With the sound of cheers still fresh in his mind, he was confronted with the same intransigence and skepticism from owners and managers who knew his talents but were deathly afraid of his unpredictable eccentricity. The Earl of Eldon remained a committed friend and supporter, however, and early in '56 he caught word of a swinging party scene that seemed just perfect for His Highness.

"Bongomania" it was called, and it amounted to a floating celebration of rhythm – specifically, of the bongo beat that was then the hippest craze of the Hollywood hotshots. A promoter was renting a variety of halls and theaters for Saturday night parties that attracted 600-700 of Hollywood's swingin-est citizens, including a smattering of 'hot' celebrities like Marlon Brando. The events were simple enough: a little jazz, a few bongo players, and 600 snake-dancing bongomaniacs stoned to the gills on anything they could get their hands on.

The first night Lord Buckley and Eldon attended a session, it was held at the former *Preston Sturgess Players Theater* on Sunset, a beautiful building packed full of revelers. It didn't take long for His Highness and the Earl to pick up on what was going down, and to realize the organization was so loose, it begged for royal supervision. Lord Buckley quickly approved of his friend's suggestion that what the show needed most was the lift only Buckley could give, and His Lordship persuaded Eldon to get up onstage and introduce him.

"Ladies and gentlemen," the Earl announced over the babble of the crowd, "we are fortunate tonight to have in our midst the incomparable Lord Buckley. If we encourage him a bit, maybe he'll come up here and lay something down for us."

Buckley dutifully answered the call of his audience, and laid down his standard jazz show at the time, consisting of *The Nazz, Jonah, Nero*, and an assortment of others. The audience, his timing, the environment – everything went right. "He was the gas of the night," according to Eldon. Apparently the promoter thought so too, as he asked Buckley to become a regular performer.

For three weeks the party cruised along in good form, until finally the promoter decided that he and Buckley should be a team and create their own happenings. It seemed like a reasonable idea, and so the *Hollywood Athletic Club* was rented and a jazz combo was hired to supplement the bongo players. The show came off as planned, except for a few irritating details. A huge nine-foot drum, on loan from a local dealer, was stolen from in front of the *Club*. And the box office, manned by Eldon, came up a little short in its receipts – much to the consternation of the promoter. Anyway, that was the end of Buckley's *Bongomania* involvement, sending Eldon and him back out scuffling for jobs once more.

Money was virtually nonexistent in early '56, and anything he did earn, or borrow, was instantly spent for whatever necessity was most pressing at the moment. By

April it became obvious to Buckley that even the tiny
Crackerbox Palace was becoming too much of a financial
burden; then, too, he had a friend – Bob Dewitt – who told
him about the wonders of nearby Topanga Canyon, where
Dewitt lived with his wife and family. Isolated, serene, and yet
close to the L.A. action and inhabited by a small group of
beatnik types, the Canyon was the ideal alternative to the
high-paced hustle of Hollywood.

So the Royal Court packed up and moved once more,
this time to a house so tiny it made the Crackerbox look like a
real palace. Tucked away at the end of a narrow winding road
in lush surroundings, the house was one of several small
cabins that dotted the hillside. "Hobbit houses," Princess
Laurie describes them, "about 15 x 20 feet in size." Theirs
had red velvet wallpaper.

Soon after the Buckleys moved in, DeWitt opened a
cafe´ and real estate office not far below them that became a
meeting place for the local bohemian population, and a series
of Sunday tailgate meetings of the area families evolved into a
more organized venture that fulfilled the plans made two
years earlier at Whitley Terrace: The Church of the Living
Swing.

For years, Lord Buckley had given considerable
thought to religious and philosophical questions, but had not

incorporated those thoughts into his personal life much beyond his translations. A pamphlet from Henry Miller describing the tale of Nunez Cabez de Vaca, *"The Gasser,"* had included a description of *'The Power Within'* and had spurred Buckley's interest in faith healing and other related spiritualistic phenomena. It was His Lordship's belief, however, that entertainment was a necessary component of religion and that the theater was, in fact, a religious experience.

"The Theater," Lord Buckley explained, "is in itself a church. The Theater is really a religious institution because it presents life itself, in all its beauty and in all its rhythm, and it gives the people the opportunity to analyze life, and look at life, and see it flowing before their very eyes. And it's a very, very profound work. When you walk into a theater, right away you feel that it's a meeting of the people to receive the great reflection of the warm love of life through the talents and the arts of the individual."

The Church of the Living Swing was Lord Buckley's interpretation of the ideal melding of religion and entertainment. Hundreds of his neighbors and friends turned out for the service, though most, if not all, were unaware of what awaited them.

Inside DeWitt's building, they found a scene even the most travelled and sophisticated among them must have thought extraordinary. The air was full of pot smoke as the congregation sat on railroad tie benches and watched one of the first oil on glass light shows they had ever seen. A belly dancer moved to the beat laid down by the house jazz band, as Lady Buckley hurried here and there making sure all went well, dressed, according to one source, in an outfit befitting Gloria Swanson. The audience was a diverse and highly original group, ranging from local beatniks, to junkies, hookers, and religious liberals. Booze was passed around to wash down the chili and rolls that formed the communal food supply, and the atmosphere was free, relaxed, and yet attentive.

Attention was concentrated, for the most part, on Lord Buckley, whose performances that day of *"The Nazz,"* *"Jonah,"* and *"The Hip Gan"* were described as "spellbinding." Putting his oratorial skills to best use, and drawing on every ounce of his showbiz acumen, Buckley brought to life the religious aspects of his translations by imbuing them with his own magic. For many in attendance, it was the first time they had ever paid such close attention to the old religious tales, and for most everyone it was the first time they had truly enjoyed the experience.

Some thought the atmosphere to be sacrilegious, but they were a tiny minority. Others, including the police, considered the meeting to be illegal, and while the service was in full swing the vice squad raided the place. There were several arrests, and the cops thought they'd stumbled upon a major discovery when a Buckley friend, known as "The Kingpin" for his drug dealings, was found at the meeting. But Buckley himself was able to talk his way out of the bust, contending he was merely the preacher and what his flock chose to do was their own business. Apparently hard feelings arose because His Highness escaped prosecution, and rumors were circulated that Buckley had turned on his sources to avoid the bust. Few believed the charges – even the 'Kingpin' remained a friend – but the raid served to close the Church anyway.

The Buckleys only lived at the miniscule Topanga Canyon cabin for another few weeks, as Lady Buckley determined that nothing could keep her in a house the size of a prison cell. Reactivating her talents as a professional dancer, Lady B. sought out ballet students, saving the money from her teaching to get a new place to live. Buckley, meanwhile, appeared at small clubs whenever he could get gigs, and made do as best he could on the home front. But sometimes not even bravado and positive thinking could overcome the hard reality of poverty.

Shopping at the small *Topanga Market* just down the hill, Buckley picked up a grocery basket and carefully chose a number of goods he knew his family needed. He moved confidently to the check-out counter, where he informed the shop owner of the advantages of offering His Lordship temporary credit. Unfortunately, the owner didn't see the situation the same way, and he refused Buckley's request. With a surprised and disgusted look, Buckley replaced every item he'd picked up, and then returned to the cash register to buy just a pack of cigarettes. "That man is as square as an ice cube," His Highness later told Bob DeWitt, and he avoided the store for the remainder of his Topanga stay.

As soon as Lizbeth had saved enough money and was able to find a new home, the family moved again, this time to Pasadena. Gene Norman, a d.j. and show promoter in the Pasadena area, had booked Buckley into several of his jazz shows over the previous few weeks, and the new house was not only convenient but at least temporarily affordable. Lyle Griffin, an old friend of Buckley's dating back to his days in the late 30's playing the *Hollywood Cafe*, came onto the scene once again with his tape recorder and ideas for some record releases, attending virtually all Buckley's appearances during mid '56 — taping everything. With an "All Star Jazz Band" consisting of Dodo Marmarosa on piano, Lucky Thompson on tenor sax, and led by Griffin, Buckley recorded an original piece called *"Flight Of The Saucer,"* a '45' released on the *Hip*

Records label. Part One catalogued the saucer's journey to Mars, while Part II took it to Jupiter.

Buckley was assigned the title "Professor of Hipology."

In May, 1956, Lord Buckley became a contributing writer for *DIG Magazine*, "America's Coolest Teenage Magazine." His initial feature was a hip version of Columbus discovering America: "This is the tale of a Genoese called the Hip Chris," it began. "This swingin' Portugese cat used to sit on the dock and dig the Aqua Scene, the flippin', jumpin', stompin' billows of the Realm of Neptunareni."

The magazine was dedicated "for teenagers only," and most of the articles reflected that bent. "Are You Shy?", "Tattoos Are for The Birds," and "Things That Boys Don't Like About Girls" were some of the journalistic offerings, while a photo layout displayed the latest variants of the ducktail haircut. Buckley's article stood out conspicuously as the most distinctly hip material in the magazine, and also the most traditionally educational. Again, His Lordship had mixed learning with entertainment, and pulled it off. He spoke their new language and the teens (or at least some of them) understood perfectly.

Out in Pasadena, Buckley attracted the same crowds of people he always had, as friends came to visit virtually every day. One of those was fellow comedian Redd Foxx, who Buckley had known for years. Redd was experiencing some hard times too, and was driving an old car so beat-up that "it didn't have any first or second gear, and there wasn't enough power in third to get up the hill. So I turned around, put it in reverse, and backed up the street to the house."

Buckley, always a free spirit with a great love for the human body, met Redd at the door stark naked. "Nothing's really ever hidden here," His Lordship explained, "so there's no need for hiding anything." The two men ate spaghetti, talked, and got high on "African ganja." "We had both gone pretty much the same route; we'd said it all before. The Fifties were changing times. Times of rebellion. But Buckley did too much too soon. He scared people. He was so original and flighty that it was hard for people to keep up." A few months later, Foxx came back to see Buckley again, but he was gone.

Aside from his concert dates with Gene Norman's gigs, Buckley was landing occasional short stints at clubs all around the city. At *Jazz City* he played on a bill with Billie Holliday, and at the *Renaissance*, he was a featured act. At one show, Benny Shapiro, a co-owner of the club, was thrown into a nervous frenzy when showtime came and went without any sign of Buckley. When His Lordship finally appeared, the audience was just beginning to file out, and Shapiro started to lace into Richard for his negligence.

Unaffected by the negative vibes, Buckley grabbed his boss's hand in a friendly shake and began to warmly extoll the virtues of a beautiful night. After a few tense moments, Buckley defused the situation, though his reputation in the local entertainment biz took another severe beating.

His reputation as one of Hollywood's most colorful characters, however, was constantly reinforced both in the upper and lower circles of L.A. Dining with a group at *Chasen's* – one of the finest restaurants in the city – Buckley belatedly 'discovered' that he was without sufficient funds to cover the somewhat extravagant bill. Spying Humphrey Bogart nearby, Lord B. had the waiter bring the check to Bogie, who was gracious enough to pay it.

At the other end of the spectrum, after late night performances on Western Ave., Buckley and Mel Welles would travel to the *Hollywood Ranch Market* where "all the denizens of the street" hung out to munch on the 10 cent hamburgers. In his white tails, Buckley shone in the dingy Market, as he laid philosophical pearls on the assembled multitude using the street language they understood best. Buckley's reputation as *The Pied Piper of Hollywood* came from such encounters, a reputation of endearment to the street people, of derision to some of the local upper crust.

Although appearing much the same to those who only saw him infrequently, friends of His Highness recall that

Buckley was evolving, in his private, personal thoughts and reflections.

"He was gathering his philosophy," recalls Robert Mitchum, "getting into meditation and even astral projection." His philosophical and spiritualistic nature was expanding, becoming ever more important to His Lordship even as his life continued on its uncharted, free-form path.

In September, Lord Buckley was booked into Montreal, doing his old 4-person pantomime routine in a show called *'Gayety.'* In October, Buckley began a series of hip shows at the *L.A. Carmel Theater*, at 8613 Santa Monica Blvd. The 1:30 a.m. shows were advertised as *"His Royal Highness Lord Buckley In Concert And Hip Recital,"* and played weekly until Halloween – October 31.

Always interested in the latest technological advances and newest head-trips, His Highness persuaded the Air Force a short time thereafter to allow him to ride in a jet airplane by using the military contacts he'd made from his numerous benefit performances. Travelling to Louisiana, Buckley took a short but speedy ride in the plane and emerged "green" but impressed.

Laying it all out in hip, *"Buckley Takes a Jet Ride"* was featured in the December issue of *Dig.*

At the same time Buckley was soaring above the clouds, a film called *'Rock All Night'* was in pre-production with a part especially designed for Lord Buckley. As Mel Welles recalls: "He'd won a part in a picture called *'Rock All Night,'* playing Sir Bop, about an agent who talked only in hip talk with white hair and a white moustache and a white beard. He wore a beret and was very flamboyant and handled all the rock musicians. It was a remake of an award-winning movie called *The Little Guy.*

"Dick Clark played the Little Guy. Roger Corman bought the property, turned it into *'Rock All Night'* with the Platters and a number of other hot groups. And then Buckley disappeared. It was one of those time that he just dropped off the face of the earth, resurfacing about three months later down south. So, at the last minute there was no one to play the part, so I dyed my hair, my moustache, and my beard white, put a beret on, and played Sir Bop."

It was classic Buckley. Just as things seemed to be heating up for him professionally, just as the family had once again found a comfortable home, he decided to leave California and head for Florida. Why? According to Lizbeth, a friend of His Lordship stopped by and described the Miami scene as the nearest thing to paradise, capturing Buckley's imagination. Other considerations be damned. The Buckleys were moving.

Again.

His Highness flew on ahead, hoping to scout up some gigs and a place to stay so he could be working when the family pulled in. Lizbeth and the kids packed up all their belongings and crammed them into their Buick and a trailer they pulled. The drive took longer than expected when the car broke down in Jackson, Mississippi, and repairs necessitated a five-day layover. Yet when they arrived at last in Florida, Buckley hadn't found a job. His friend, Capt. Jack, provided a place to stay, but the plethora of gigs he had anticipated didn't materialize.

For over a month the Buckleys lived with Capt. Jack, and after a while Lord Buckley began to find jobs in small private clubs. They ran into several old acquaintances in Miami, including Harry the Hipster *("Who Put the Benzedrine In Mrs. Murphy's Ovaltine?"),* the Vagabonds, and Princess Lily (Tubby Boots.) Visiting Harry one night in a tough little nightclub just off the beach, Lord and Lady Buckley saw one of the customers throw a glass that smashed against Harry's piano. Harry kept on playing, his fingers bleeding, until Lord Buckley stopped him and Lizbeth helped tend his hands.

Unknown to His Lordship, another old friend, Faith Dane, was living not too far away and happened to see his appearance advertised in the paper. Just a few days earlier,

Faith, a trumpet playing comedienne and actress who appeared in '*Gypsy*,' had stumbled upon a spectacular mansion that belonged to a wealthy eccentric. The House, located right on the beach on Coiling St., was empty, and Faith and her husband of two days, John O'Fallon, moved in.

When the O'Fallons stopped by the theater to visit Buckley, little did they realize that by inviting His Lordship and family to visit them the next day for a swim, they'd be turning their beautiful home over to the Royal Court. But when Lord Buckley saw the two-story, Spanish-style hacienda, with 15 rooms, a circular driveway, and a huge ballroom complete with marble floor, there was no denying him. He wanted to live there. He was going to live there. It was even more spectacular than Whitley Terrace, even more fitting as a home for the Court.

But Faith knew the Buckleys were "precarious people," and she insisted that Richard come to an arrangement before she would even consider letting them move in. Buckley agreed to her demands, and even had a friend bring a check to pay the initial deposit. Several days later, by the time the check bounced, the O'Fallons knew they were in for more than they'd bargained for.

The O'Fallons were young and very much in love. In fact, John had left the seminary where he was studying to be a priest to marry Faith, but no marriage only a few days old was ready for Lord Buckley. In no time he was referring to the house as "my castle," and his ever-present friends were on the scene day and night.

"His groupies ate us out of everything," Faith says, "and I had to go back to work just to feed them all." Of course, some of Buckley's friends, like Tony Bennett (who took *Ballet for Living* lessons from Lizbeth – a combination of dance, posture, exercise, and attitude) were welcome. But many, many others were the sort who showed up for the fun and food and contributed virtually nothing. It was much the same as other Royal Courts, but this time His Lordship didn't have the money to support the happenings.

Financial worries and lack of privacy put a tremendous strain on the O'Fallons, and the pressure began to eat away at their relationship. When Faith saw the problems developing to a point where her marriage was threatened, she asked the Buckleys to leave. "They wouldn't even talk to me," Faith says. "By that time they felt so at home, and had so many friends visiting, that they were indignant I should ask them to leave. Lizbeth even suggested that John and I go on a cruise!"

For His Lordship and family, Miami was a dream come true. A host of good friends came down to visit, and the Florida Court kept up a wild and carefree existence in the big, beautiful mansion. Buckley landed occasional local gigs, including a January booking at the *Pagoda Room* of the Saxony Hotel in which he was billed as "Sir Richard the Riotous Rogue," and he even worked several weeks in Nassau, the Bahamas.

But much of the time he had free to himself, and the children saw more of their father than ever before. Despite the fact they were only 6 and 8, Richard taught them both to drive in the large circular driveway. According to young Richard, "he told us to aim the hood ornament at the middle of the road. If we had to go between two things, he told us to size up the dashboard and decide if it would go between the obstacles. If it would, the car would make it too." Little Richard was so small he could barely see over the steering wheel, but he practiced anyway. One morning Lizbeth looked out from the balcony that overlooked the driveway to see the car circling the driveway – apparently driverless. Her screams brought out Buckley, who explained that everything was okay, it was just their 6-year-old son taking the car out for a spin.

"We used to do funny things," Laurie remembers. "We used to have to walk down this long walkway to empty the garbage, and at night it was real dark. It was a long, long aisle with a cement wall on both sides. My dad was on one side of the wall, where we couldn't see him. Well, we were hurrying real fast, trying to empty the garbage and get back, when Dad jumped up in the moonlight, raised his arms wide and growled 'AAARGH!' I mean to tell you, we just screamed with terrified delight... and ran. He just scared the hell out of us! And he laughed; he just thought that was the funniest thing, and we loved it, too – after we reached the house."

At night, if circumstances permitted, Buckley liked to hang out at the small beachfront clubs. Meeting people was one of his great joys, and one of those he met in early '56 was Toni Goldman. "Here comes Miss Skinny of 1956," he announced upon seeing her, "you could turn her around and thread her like a needle." Luckily, Toni knew of Buckley through Larry Storch, and rather than take offense, she laughed. "Buckley was somewhat of a loner in the clubs," she says. "He was into meditation, e.s.p., and yoga. And he had a habit of emptying cigarettes and filling them with marijuana; but no one seemed the wiser. You couldn't tell if he was high or sober because he could always hold an intellectual conversation.

"He mixed with black people, which was a no-no in Miami, but he loved them, and all jazz musicians. And when he performed, and the people were cool enough to dig it, there wasn't a sound in the room. He talked so fast you almost didn't want to laugh because you didn't want to miss the next thing he said."

In February, Buckley flew out to Las Vegas once again to appear at the San Marino Hotel's *Carnivale Lounge* with Sandra Barton. Vegas held a special fascination for Lord Buckley. Ever since the early Forties he had worked the desert resort, and through the years he had seen it grow from a dusty railroad stop to an up-and-coming vacation mecca. Not only did he foresee the potential of the city, but so many of his old friends either played or visited Vegas regularly that it was the perfect spot to see them all again. So, taking virtually all the money he earned as well as anything he could borrow, His Lordship made the unprecedented move of buying a house on the outskirts of town.

Returning to Miami, Buckley learned of an upcoming *Ziegfeld Follies* tour, and through a stroke of luck both he and Lizbeth were booked into the show. Lady Buckley was hired as a showgirl, and so in mid-summer she went on ahead to New York, where the Follies were organizing, to be fitted for costumes. Buckley and the kids followed a couple of weeks later.

In New York, Lord Jocko became the babysitter while the senior Buckleys rehearsed, preparing for a long road trip that was supposed to include both East and West coasts as well as Canada. Buckley was one of the headliners, along with Kaye Ballard, and Micki Marlowe, and he worked several comedic skits with other cast members.

Opening on Friday, September 13, 1957, in Toronto, the show was an immediate critical success. Billed as Lord Buckley, His Highness brought not only comedic skills to the production, but considerable dramatic flair also. His children were frequent visitors to the show, usually sitting up in the balcony with the producer's kid watching every move and participating vicariously in every scene.

Sometimes the participation became more than vicarious, and on several occasions Laurie got into disagreements with the producer's daughter when she sang along with show numbers. A new addition to the entourage helped make the daily shows and train trips more tolerable by introducing a little excitement and luxury into the Buckleys' lives. Ron Asher, known as *"Asher The Dasher"* by nearly everyone, was a wealthy businessman who lived at the top of the classy *Essex House* in New York, and just happened to be infatuated with Micki Marlowe as well as fascinated by Lord Buckley.

Wherever the Follies played, everyone kept an eye out for the Dasher, and more often than not he would appear with gifts for everyone. The kids were the object of much of his generosity, receiving toys, cameras, shoes, and finely-tailored clothes at nearly every visit. After the gifts, the Dasher would take the whole group out to the fanciest restaurant in whatever town they happened to be in and treat them to anything they desired.

But Ron wasn't always there, and even when he was Lord Buckley could be counted on to come up with his own contribution to the festivities. Kaye Ballard remembers His Lordship calling up at 3 a.m. on more than one occasion with the bouncy announcement "Spaghetti Time!" and instructing her to be ready in 15 minutes for the car that would come to pick her up. No excuses or explanations were accepted. The group would meet for a late dinner/early spaghetti breakfast and talk and party until daybreak, with His Lordship leading the discussions and providing impetus if the proceedings lagged.

The show continued for nearly three months, touring from Canada down through much of the Eastern seaboard, playing anywhere from a few days to a couple of weeks in cities of all sizes. The show was well-received wherever it played, but the West Coast segment of the tour failed to materialize and in December the show closed.

After a few months, with nothing to keep them in the East and a new home awaiting them in Vegas, the Buckleys packed up once more and began the long trek West in a friend's car. Lord Buckley went on ahead to play the *El Rancho* with Candy Barr. When the family finally arrived in Las Vegas about a week later, they were anxious to see the home His Lordship had found, the one and only house he'd ever purchased. As they passed through town and began to head out San Francisco (now Sahara) Blvd., however, they were somewhat distressed to see the gradual disappearance of all signs of civilization, giving way to the vast, hot desert. Finally, about four miles from the hub of Las Vegas activity and over a mile from the last groupings of houses, the Buckleys pulled up to a small ranch-style home in the middle of nowhere.

It took a bit of adjustment for Lizbeth and the kids to alter their living habits to match the requirements of their new home. For one thing, the nearest house was barely within view, and the last few miles of road leading out to the ranch were unpaved. The house was surrounded by literally hundreds of mattresses the Army had supposedly dumped out there, and so the house was immediately nicknamed 'The Mattress Mine.'

There was no public electricity, and so a generator had to be fired up in a nearby pumphouse to provide running water. Although they had arrived in the relative comfort of early spring, nights were surprisingly cool, while daytime temperatures would hit 120° in just five or six months. There was no telephone, and even if there was, there wasn't anyone to call. Fashion, at least off the Strip, consisted of blue jeans and boots. It was definitely not New York.

But Buckley loved the heat, and the open spaces, and – according to Eldon – he looked forward to kicking back for a while and just playing "the barracuda," borrowing or conning money from the vast numbers of entertainment friends who would pass through town.

Clothing was an unnecessary encumbrance way out in the middle of nowhere, and the endless empty desert was perfect for testing one's lungs and perfecting vocal projection. It was not unusual to hear His Lordship orating to the cactus, announcing in a shout that could've been heard for miles – if there'd been anyone there to hear – "Eisenhower is a fag! And Mamie is a lesbian!"

With the creativity that marked any iteration of the Royal Court, Lord Buckley and family used the resources at their disposal to create a suitable environment. Bama, who had come out from New York, helped for the first week or so, but the aridity and rural atmosphere quickly sent him on his way. Using the 4-500 mattresses strewn across the desert, the Buckleys created a mattress walkway out to the pumphouse, and a circular patio with outrageous high-backed mattress chairs. They built a fireplace in the middle of the patio, where nightly bonfires were held.

At night, with the fire smoldering, the family and any friends who had managed to brave the trek out into the desert would sit in the silent blackness and look out over an unobstructed view of the Strip, marveling at the necklace of brilliant lights that seemed to hover above the endless sand and scrub. Far to the east, near Sunrise Mountain, the town burned its trash, sending tongues of orange flame into the clear night air. The silence and the blackness were nearly complete, except for glimmering bands of stars that swept across the skies.

Inside the Mattress Mine, Lizbeth painted the floors in brilliant splashes of color, and the walls were dotted with slogans and sayings that His Lordship pulled out of the innumerable books and articles he read. One of Bob DeWitt's huge murals was given a place of honor, and the collected mementoes of decades on the road were scattered throughout the house.

Though gigs at the *El Rancho* and *El Cortez* hotels brought in occasional paychecks, much of His Lordship's income was acquired from gifts and '*loans*' he persuaded fellow performers to *donate*. Some entertainers were perfectly understanding and willing to cooperate; others were less cooperative. One night at the *Frontier Hotel*, Dean Martin accepted His Lordship most graciously, bowing formally and advancing $50 toward the cause.

Tony Curtis, on the other hand, a long-time friend dubbed *The Prince of The Atomic Age*, declined to contribute. Whether it was Curtis' snub or not, no one seems sure, but Buckley fell into a petulant mood and was later asked to leave after throwing silver dollars in the casino.

The recipients of a great deal of His Highness's considerable free time were the children, who finally had a Daddy like the other kids. Or almost. He'd drive them into town in their big, black '51 Chrysler convertible with Laurie, Richard, and the kids from a new family in the neighborhood, the Reynolds, all sitting in the back of the car singing *"Blue Skies."* On the way back, the kids were allowed to sit on the hood and hold on over the bumpy dirt roads. At night, sitting around the bonfire, Buckley told endless stories about himself, his friends, and imaginary characters from storybooks and his own imagination. In a twinkling, he transformed himself from a Biblical character to a human choo-choo engine, with all the kids grabbing on behind and following his piercing train whistle throughout the house and surrounding desert. At bedtime, Laurie and Richard were always prime targets for a thorough tickling, leaving them gasping for breath and sore from laughing.

In addition to Art and Vera Reynolds and their kids, who moved in just a half-mile away, Buckley's regular visitors included the Earl of Eldon, who with his wife Maria had moved to Vegas when they found out Lord Buckley was there, and the Kestersons, Ding and Bonnie. Ding was a professional musician who had heard Buckley on record; when they met they hit it off immediately. Buckley would stop by, (once wearing leotards with a jock strap on the outside), and he and Lizbeth would rap and get high with the new members of the Court. "He told me one story," Ding recalls, "about when he was with Ed Sullivan at a Navy base in Virginia. There were 1100 low-ranking officers taking a test in an auditorium, and Buckley was backstage casing out the place he was going to work. He peeks through the curtain and sees these officers taking the exam, and he starts delivering a dissertation on the perils of 'going over the hill.' He told me all 1100 had to take the test over again."

Rather quickly, Lord Buckley became a well-known figure around Las Vegas, as a celebrity and as Chairman of the Public Relations Committee of the *George Washington Carver Memorial Institute*. Lord and Lady Buckley were frequent visitors to the Strip, and were often received with a dignitary's welcome. For instance, whenever Ed Sullivan brought his revue to town, the Buckleys would always be seated in a front

booth and introduced from the audience. Lady Buckley
contributed her share to their notoriety, appearing with His
Lordship in a variety of gowns ranging from designer
originals to the orange jumpsuits used at a nearby titanium
mine – with an ermine jacket as eye-popping accessory.

Virtually everyone in the business either knew Buckley
or had heard him, so reunions and long-overdue first
meetings were regular events. But not everything ran
smoothly, not by any means. Buckley's income, both earned
and *acquired*, barely covered the essentials at home. And a
devastating fire nearly destroyed the Mattress Mine just a few
months after they moved in. Because they had no electricity,
the household used Coleman and kerosene lamps to provide
light, and so they stored kerosene in a container in the
kitchen. One night, the container accidently spilled and
kerosene spread across the kitchen floor, moving in an instant
under the butane refrigerator where the pilot light ignited it.
The tinder-dry wood and belongings burst into flames that
engulfed the kitchen in seconds and began to spread into the
living room.

Little Richard, just seven years old, raced out to the
pumphouse and turned on the water pump so they could
hose down the remainder of the house and keep it from
catching fire too. Despite the flames soaring into the sky,
none of the nearby neighbors came to assist the Buckleys,

since those who saw the blaze thought it was just another of the regular bonfires.

As the fire burned, Laurie sat on the ground outside crying. "Now we'll have to start all over again," she sobbed, and for a while it looked like that would be the case. But with a good dousing and a little luck, they stopped the fire before it spread beyond the living room.

Undaunted by the setback, Lord and Lady Buckley spent a couple of days sifting through the rubble and reorganizing the remaining rooms, after which the family just moved back in. The smell of smoke was heavy everywhere, but the bedrooms were otherwise intact. Buckley's insurance man came on the scene remarkably quickly, and in less than three weeks the reconstruction was complete. His Lordship suggested to the carpenters that they leave the roof open so he could take advantage of the spectacular night skies from the comfort of his living room, but he was persuaded to close it up.

A few days after the fire, some old friends of the family showed up at the Mattress Mine unexpectedly. Although they had no knowledge of the fire, they had brought several cases of soup, some pewter goblets, and several oil paintings as gifts for His Highness and family, and their arrival was welcomed as an example of fortuitous happenstance.

Once it became widely known that Lord Buckley had set up permanent residence in Las Vegas, the steady stream of friends began as it always did. Some came to dry out from alcohol, others to see how a longtime city dweller could possibly adjust to the desert life. But most came to just talk, and get high, and laugh. They found an older Buckley, 52, and a man considerably more settled and philosophical. Not that His Lordship had become a new person, but perhaps for the first time his mellow, reflective side began to take precedence over his lifelong craziness. In fact, according to Mel Welles, "his main ambition became to score big and give his family some semblance of security."

Correspondence from Henry Miller helped keep up His Lordship's spirits, and visits from his friends made the Vegas scene a *swingin' gasser*. They'd sit and talk into the early hours of the morning, reminiscing, planning, joking, and rapping down a host of topics from politics to UFO's.

With the U.S. Explorer satellite just launched to join two Russian Sputniks already in orbit, space was one of the more recurrent themes for discussion, and with no shortage of people who claimed to have seen flying saucers, the talks got pretty far-out indeed. Whatever the subject, Lord Buckley had more than likely either read or heard about it, and with a total lack of taboos, no subject was eliminated off-hand.

One of the many local residents who met Lord Buckley for the first time after he moved to Vegas was a 25-year-old would-be theatrical agent named Lewis Foremaster. Like many others, Foremaster's first knowledge of His Lordship came through records he had heard, and then via shows he saw in local clubs. After one such gig at the *El Rancho*, Lewis introduced himself to His Lordship and was invited out to the Mattress Mine to meet the Court and share with them experiences, fellowship, and anything else that might be required. Lewis was fascinated and impressed by Lord Buckley's originality and style, and as soon as he could arrange it, he drove his big Oldsmobile out to the ranch "to listen and get high."

After that first meeting came many more, and soon Prince Lewis had become Buckley's assistant, valet, chauffeur – what have you. Lewis's family owned one of Vegas' largest dairies at the time, and after hearing a variety of Buckley's characters Prince Lewis was convinced His Lordship would be just perfect for an advertisement promoting Arden's Medigold Milk. So Lord Buckley wrote and recorded a series of hip radio commercials that extolled the virtues of Medigold milk indirectly via stories and monologues. In one,

Buckley insists to a cow that she "Let it down" and so
produce the superb milk that went into Arden's. In another, a
humorous story about a dog and a horse concludes with the
speaker needing a big glass of milk to cool himself. All the
spots were captivating and entertaining.

Unfortunately, when the Foremasters listened to the
recordings they immediately wondered aloud what the hell
His Lordship was talking about. Once again, the straight
world was unable to see past the structure of Lord Buckley's
words to the images they contained, and so the recordings
remained unreleased and Medigold remained on its previous
course.

As the year progressed, Lord Buckley began to itch for
the stage and the lifestyle it had once – and hopefully would
again – provided for him and his family. Recovering from a
broken arm suffered when a drunk grabbed his foot while he
was demonstrating how to leap over a neighborhood bar, His
Highness was anxious to get back on the boards. Nearly every
day he'd send little Richard, then eight, down to the mailbox a
quarter mile away to get the day's mail, looking for news of a
gig, or word from Henry Miller, Ed Sullivan, or any of his
other friends. Richard would jump into the Chrysler and,
straining to see over the steering wheel, drive down to the
box and back with the deliveries, being careful to avoid any

small animals in his path – most especially Miss Crazy Blues, the family's newly-adopted pet dog.

Although the steady flow of friends both in and out of the business, including Johnathan Winters, Robin Ford, and many, many others, kept His Lordship busy and motivated, the lack of serious job offers hurt his pride and confidence. An October gig at the *Riverside* in Reno proved he still had the same magnetism to move audiences at will, but it also reemphasized his inability to gain wide acceptance for the hip act – his prime consideration. As winter crept up on him, he decided to try a road trip to Los Angeles, where he hoped to raise enough money for a real Christmas, complete with a tree and presents. The family had done without before, and although His Lordship made it seem "so beautiful we hardly realized we didn't have a tree," according to Laurie, it was a bad scene for Buckley, one he didn't want duplicated.

So Lord Buckley summoned Prince Lewis and suggested they go "off busking" to L.A., and Lewis prepared to set out at once. His Lordship had nothing firm awaiting him in the city, but he had friends who were more than willing to house him and Prince Lewis while he searched around for jobs. Jack and Betty Kuhn gave Buckley free run of the house and he used their telephone as if it was his private business line. Ed Sullivan had promised His Lordship

a show appearance for the end of the year, and he eagerly
awaited that call. Buckley might have considered travelling
out to N.Y. to wait for the appearance, but Sullivan
persuaded him not to come to the City until just before the
show so he wouldn't get into any trouble. There were many
temptations in New York, and Buckley was too well-known
to slip into the City and stay for any length of time without
His people finding him.

Then too, as Sullivan explained, as soon as he
announced that His Highness was scheduled to appear on the
show, Ed received all sorts of phone calls from people
claiming Buckley owed them money. So the Kuhn's house
was an ideal base of operations as Buckley sought out any and
all gigs in the surrounding area. If he was depressed or in bad
spirits, he never showed it to the Kuhns, for according to
Betty "he never stopped and kept everyone else going." He
frightened the old woman living next door by stepping
outside in his shorts and t-shirt and practicing his Tarzan yell,
and then won her over with a charming pitch that convinced
her he was not only perfectly sane, but a suave gentleman at
that. A cuckoo clock in the house constantly interrupted his
monologues, so he timed his stories to pause or finish on the
quarter hour. The local population soon heard of his
presence, and admirers stopped by to meet him and chat.

One group who arrived while Jack and Richard were out, greeted him with a burning joint, prompting His Lordship to assume the role of a complete stranger to marijuana with questions like, "What is this stuff?" and "How do you roll it up like this?" A few expert tokes revealed his true character.

One evening when Lewis couldn't chauffeur him, Buckley took a cab to a gig at a small club on the outskirts of Camp Pendleton. "What do you know about this place?" he asked the driver, attempting to initiate some friendly conversation. "Oh, it's a nice enough place," the driver answered, "we don't get many niggers in there." After a short pause, Buckley agreed. "It's sure a good thing they don't let none of those goddamn niggers in there." The first time he repeated the statement, the driver smiled and grunted his approval. The next time he repeated it, somewhat colder and harder, the driver didn't respond at all. After several more repetitions, each colder and harder than the first, the driver was driving abnormally fast with sweat pouring down the side of his face. When he finally let Buckley out at the club, His Lordship paid the man and then leaned in close: "Sure is a good thing... isn't it?"

"Yeh, yeh, sure... I mean... take it easy," the driver mumbled as he gunned off into the night.

Such gigs were infrequent at best, but Lord Buckley was not the sort to allow a temporary lack of paying engagements to interrupt his daily regimen of performing. His impromptu performances in public places are legendary. Spying William Holden in a restaurant, Buckley announced, at the top of his voice, "Well, well, if it isn't William Holden. But the question is, is William holdin'?" The actor smiled as knowledgeable people snickered, and Buckley sat down to eat as though he hadn't said a word. And in supermarkets all across the country, there were check-out girls who became part of the Buckley world as he broke into improvised scenes while in line to pay for his shopping.

It was nothing for His Lordship to include strangers in a skit they didn't even know was occurring, for wherever he found an audience, they found a performer.

While he stayed in the L.A. area searching for jobs, Buckley made frequent nightly visits to Long Beach – less than an hour's drive south – to satisfy both his appetite for performing and his all-too-real appetite for good food. An old friend and longtime musician, Charlie Ray, owned a club located just four blocks from the ocean called *"The Twin Flames,"* and there a host of fine entertainers – including Anita O'Day, Julie London, and June Christie – performed and partook of the 80-cent cook-your-own steak dinners. At the time, the break-in drummer and parttime bartender was a young man named Tony Albanese, who later went on to own a series of clubs including the *Hullabaloo* in Hollywood. But in 1958, Tony was working the *Flames* when Buckley began his nightly visits.

"When Buckley walked in," he remembers, "that would be it. Charlie would see him from across the room and gather up all the maracas and cabasas and anything else he'd passed out, and that was it, I mean it was his room, he could do whatever he'd want. He'd walk in with one of his famous, 'Charlie, my good man' openers and go right into a bit and Charlie would pick up on it, and before you knew it, he'd do an album. He'd sit at the piano bar and they'd be bringing him his drinks and he'd be sipping in-between, and whatever he'd be ordering from the cocktail waitress he'd work right into the show. Most of the time I was laughing so hard I couldn't sit up on the drum seat.

"Charlie would motion to the cocktail waitress to get him whatever he wants, and even ordering the drink would be worked into the schtick. Whatever story he'd be into from the time he hit the door he'd just go right into, 'And then the fair maiden entered' as the waitress bent over to pick up a napkin or something. He was *on* from the moment he hit the room. It wasn't one of those things where he'd come in and say hello to everybody and then sit down. From the moment he pushed open the front door, he was *on*.

"This would go on for an hour and a half, two hours, even three hours if he really got wound up! By this time everybody who's cooking their steaks have burned them, they'd leave them sitting there, and they're all huddled around this piano bar laughing like fools. Nobody had a chance to get to the cooking pit 'cause they couldn't get past the mob, the cocktail waitresses wouldn't be able to work – we made absolutely no money when he was in there at all. In his bits he'd do women's parts, men's parts, even the little kid parts – and he sounded like a little kid. When he did a little black kid, he sounded like a little black kid, and if he did an Italian little kid, he sounded like an Italian little kid.

"We'd see him just about every night for a month or so. While he was performing, one of the girls would be cooking a steak for him, and he was eating on the bar top, and having two or three drinks, but he wouldn't miss a beat. Like in one bit, when King Arthur was introducing the Chastity Belt, he'd change right in the middle of it to a black King Arthur and Lady Guinevere, and the voice'd change, and the whole scene'd change – you'd swear, if you weren't watching him, it was two different people. Now, while he's doing the bit he's eating his steak, his garbanzo beans, and he's not missing a lick on it. If he wanted another drink or something, he'd just work it into the bit – the same voice and everything. And then when he was done, he was done. He'd finish his drink and then just walk out.

"Only one time in all the times he came down to the club do I remember him getting pissed off. Charlie was trying to tell the bartender to get the cocktail waitresses in there selling, and finally he went over to the mike... and Buckley blew up. 'If you're so stupid you can't follow an artist when he's working; If your mind is so into your cash register... You can blow it out your ear!" Charlie was beat red, trying to smile, but Buckley slammed his stool on the ground and just took off out the back door. I'll tell you, in all the thousands of people I've met in this business, he's one of the few I'll always remember."

Back in L.A., a series of shows Buckley landed at the *Los Palmos* theater was cut short when complaints brought in the police. The first night it was immediately evident the program was not going to be black-tie when concert-goers were confronted by junkies nodding off in the lobby and assorted "beatnik types" passing out "all sorts of bennies." But Buckley appeared as scheduled and performed for four hours, much of the time sitting on the stage with his legs dangling over the side. Those in the small crowd who were conscious enough to pay attention applauded appreciatively, but it wasn't enough to offset the influence of a sizeable number of strung-out hipheads. The police heard about the situation and busted the place the next night.

Despite such setbacks, Lord Buckley and Lewis kept up their search for new gigs, and His Lordship accumulated a small amount of money toward his goal of a bountiful Christmas even as the season rapidly approached. Although Buckley's success was limited in his professional endeavors, he was surprisingly successful – even miraculously so – in his development of *"the power within."*

For many years Lord Buckley had believed in the principle of faith healing, and was confident if anyone had the ability to channel their innate psychic powers to the benefit of those sick or injured, it was he. In private conversations the topic came up frequently, and several friends had received "The Power" from his hands to cure a headache or other minor ache or pain. But with Betty Kuhn, His Lordship attempted to influence a considerably more dangerous malady, one that sent Betty to a specialist for diagnosis.

She had had "female troubles" for some time, but she was stunned to learn her doctor diagnosed the problem as cancer. In a conversation with His Lordship, Betty explained the circumstances and went on to detail her fears that even surgery might not completely cure her. Lord Buckley listened intently, and then explained to her his belief in "the power within."

Buckley was never so convincing as when he strongly believed in what he was discussing, and he imparted his belief to Betty while persuading her to allow him to demonstrate the technique. With "nothing to lose," she agreed.

Buckley wasn't dramatic in his demonstration. In fact, the actual implementation of the power was somewhat mundane. He simply placed his hands on her head and said a few words of suggestion. But despite the simplicity of the act, when Betty returned to her specialist for a second exam, the tests came back negative! Decades later, she still refused to deny the possibility that *The Power* had cured her.

As December began and the need to score one last solid gig became critical, the Earl of Eldon came on the scene to help Lord Buckley promote a one-nighter that would give him the money to send back to Vegas. Buckley worked a few small coffee shops before the concert to keep his chops tight and earn enough bread to keep it all together, and when it came time to get the word out about his Christmas concert, one of his employers joined with Eldon to help him out.

The three of them crashed a *Laguna Players* cast party to spread the word, and Eldon arranged for His Lordship to be introduced. Buckley was ready for the Players, and proceeded to knock out a piece he called *"The Sacred Fix"* or *"The Return of the Stranger,"* a bit in which an unctuous holy man is interrupted in the middle of a hypocritical sermon by a vision of his Savior:

"Jesus Christ: it's Jesus Christ!" the holy man shouts in embarrassment, and with that punchline the crowd roared. "He encased those people in ice," according to Eldon. The show was a success both from the theatrical and the promotional standpoints, but as Eldon remembers, it wasn't a totally pleasant evening. "He loved it. He smelled theater... but it was Laguna Theater." The phony sincerity and posturing didn't sit well with His Lordship, but he welcomed them to his own performance at the *Music Box Theater.*

The show drew well from all segments of the community, and several celebrities in the audience were treated to dramatic skits in the tradition of his old vaudeville show to complement the hip material. Perhaps he was publicly auditioning for film roles. More than likely, he was merely demonstrating his considerable dramatic prowess – especially in skits like *"The Old Man On A Park Bench"* – in front of people he knew would appreciate the technique as well as the result. In any case, he raised enough money to make Christmas a pleasant reality for his family.

When the five-hour show was over, at 2 a.m., Buckley was still flying high and went across the street with Al Frazee and Eldon to record some more material. Despite a hoarse voice, His Highness blew licks until sunrise, when his weary friends called it quits. As long as a tape recorder was on, so was Lord Buckley. They had to pull the plug to stop him.

In order to earn additional money, Lord Buckley was willing to take any and all gigs he could land. One of those gigs consisted of pitching German DKW cars at an L.A. car show. Buckley landed the job through a television host who had interviewed His Lordship and was overwhelmed; his recommendation and Buckley's dashing appearance sold the manufacturers. The day of the show, Prince Lewis delivered His Lordship to the *Pacific Auditorium* only to find a huge crowd gathered around the entranceway. Buckley directed Lewis to "press onward," and Lewis did just that – driving over the curb and through the startled crowd as police whistles screamed and people scattered everywhere. As soon as they reached the door, however, Lord Buckley hopped out and left Lewis to deal with the angry multitude.

Buckley was apparently more successful at drawing people to the DKW exhibit than in selling the cars, for although large numbers of people gathered to hear his spiel, many couldn't understand what he was saying and few inquired seriously about purchasing a model. But it was a paying gig, and the DKW people were hip enough to realize the publicity was more than worth His Lordship's fee, and so they paid him without a fuss.

Before heading East to New York for the Sullivan show he'd been awaiting, His Lordship was reunited with his son Fred for the first time in years. Fred remembers the resulting occasion vividly: "The next time I saw him I was in the Marines. It was in Los Angeles, and Buckley was appearing at the *Crescendo*. We picked up a guest who was staying with us and went to the club. He gave me a title, and she was the Countess of Somebody – I was a little bit uncomfortable with the title – I didn't know what the hell to do with it. Anyway, we're sitting ringside at a table when Buckley got up in front of the audience – unfortunately the setting was not the best from the standpoint of a concert performer, it was a social bar, lined up with people back-to-back, all chatting away, meeting and greeting each other.

"So Buckley picked up his microphone, looked around at the room and launched what turned out to be – it seemed like forever but was probably only ten minutes – a scathing attack on these people: 'How dare you while I'm performing...' It was probably one of the most uncomfortable experiences I've ever sat through – it was absolutely bananas. But the whole adventure didn't seem to bother Buckley much. He just took it all in stride, just carried on as though nothing had occurred, didn't even talk about it when he was done. It was as if it didn't even happen."

At long last, Ed Sullivan got ahold of His Lordship and told him it was all clear to come to New York to do the show. Buckley flew back, did the show, and then sent his paycheck back to Lizbeth in Las Vegas to pay the mortgage and make some repairs on the Mattress Mine before his return. However, Lizbeth had other ideas. An artist friend, Count Carlo, was in town, and Lady B. approached him about the possibility of giving art classes to locals and visitors, and so develop a constant source of income. Carlo agreed, and so Lady B. bought all the required equipment and had Art Reynolds and Ding Kesterson build all the easels they would need. For a short while all went beautifully, as everyone at the Mine was involved in art classes. But even before Lord Buckley returned, the experiment had failed to generate a life of its own and the easels were piled in a corner gathering dust.

Eldon picked Lord Buckley up at the airport upon his return, and His Lordship's first question was "Has Lady Buckley been straight? Has she been going out with other guys?" Eldon assured him that everything was cool, and drove him out to the ranch.

A small gathering celebrated his return, and midway through the party Buckley drew Eldon aside to grill him. "What the hell happened to all the money I sent back? Nothing's been done to the ranch at all!" When Eldon explained the circumstances, His Lordship shook his head in sad disbelief, but never exploded as the Earl had feared. "Buckley just swung through poverty," Eldon recalls, and though he had counted on that money, he accepted its disappearance philosophically and went back to the party. "He was an original," Eldon suggests, "a man of uncommon assets. He made us all look bad in getting the most out of life."

As it turned out, Count Carlo was in Las Vegas on a gig of his own, to open an *International Jazz Festival* in the old *San Souci* – later the *Castaways*. It wasn't a big affair, but the guests of honor on opening night were Lord and Lady Buckley. A good audience had settled into their seats as the lights dimmed and Charlie Ventura came out to open the show. Charlie walked straight across the stage and into the orchestra pit, falling hard against his side and requiring assistance to get back to his dressing room. His Lordship and Carlo followed the injured performer backstage, and found him doubled over in pain and unable to go on. Lord Buckley put his hands gently on Ventura's side and instructed Ventura to "feel the energy, feel it overcome the pain." After a few minutes, Charlie got up gingerly and went back out onstage where he received a big ovation and finished the show. After the performance, Ventura was taken to a nearby hospital where x-rays showed he had two broken ribs.

The Las Vegas home scene was firming up for Buckley, as a diesel generator brought power to the house and they truly felt at home for the first time ever. The children were enrolled at the same school for more than a few months, they knew as many locals as visiting friends, and their life consisted of more than the traditional daily parties and nightly shows. In fact, when Richard was home the whole family vacationed together, twice at nearby Bullhead City on the Colorado River where Fred's parents Paula and Tommy Russo had two boats. It was one place His Lordship could actually relax.

"This one time," Fred recalls, "the big boat was out, and I had a small boat – a little sixteen-foot rowboat with a 15 hp motor. Well, everybody decided that was great, and 'Let's all go for a boat ride.' So we all loaded up in the boat and took off down the River.

"Well, down the river was just fine – no problem at all, moving right along. But when we'd decided we'd gone far enough and should turn around and come back, it was another story. Going upstream with three adults and two

children in a sixteen-foot boat with a 15 hp motor, Buckley
turned around to me – he was really quite nice about it, he
didn't challenge my knowledge even though we weren't
making much headway – and inquired if I thought we'd make
it. I think the only thing that stopped him from hijacking the
boat at the moment was the fact that I was his son. Anyway,
he controlled any such impulses and we finally made it back."

Bullhead City was a time of relaxation and family fun,
with swimming and boating and rock collecting and lengthy
conversations to pass the time. Friends of both families
stopped by to visit, including performers such as Huntz Hall
and a small but varied assortment of Court members whose
presence always brought out the Lord in Buckley. All in all,
those days on the Colorado were probably one of the very
few times the Buckleys were able to fashion even a semblance
of a 'normal' family vacation, and they were all too brief and
fleeting. For Buckley never left his career completely behind,
and new plans for making that one big move with the hip
material dominated his thoughts.

Armed with the Frazee tapes, Lord Buckley tried to
stir up some interest in Los Angeles for further professional
recordings, and in his search for a sympathetic ear he came
across Richard Bock, a producer for the *Pacific Jazz* label.
Bock was familiar with His Lordship, having seen him at *Jazz
City* five years earlier, and was excited once again by the tapes

he heard. The two men decided a live concert recording would best capture the real Buckley, and so preparations began for a short series of shows at the *Ivar Theater*. Aside from its history for Buckley, he chose the *Ivar* because a young, up-and-coming performer by the name of Lenny Bruce had had some success there, and had told Buckley about his triumph when the two met in L.A. in '58.

Aside from show business, according to Prince Lewis, the two talked "a lot about sex and women" and seemed to hit it off quite well. They shared similar outlooks on the future of comedy – with social-consciousness an integral part of humor – and shared lifestyles that were anything but acceptable to the society they hoped to hip.

The pressure grew as the concert approached, and Buckley once again fell back into drinking to bolster his battered confidence and steel himself for what he feared might be another major letdown. So many times before it had seemed like he was finally about to make it with his hip act and every time something came up. Either he'd blown it, or the audience wasn't with it, or some other circumstance had waylaid success. This time had to be different – he was nearly 54, his hair turning white, and his family had gone without for far too long. The *Ivar* was the place, and February 12-14 the time.

Posters popped up around town quoting Frank Sinatra ("Genius"), Steve Allen ("Superb") and Ed Sullivan ("An absolute must see.") Word of mouth spread throughout the area that this concert was going to be something special, and by the night of the 12th everything was in readiness.

Just before the first show, backstage, Buckley and Fred "twisted up a little number" and chatted about the upcoming program. His Highness seated his son right onstage, where he could *feel* the applause and share the moment with Buckley. Lord Buckley was dressed in tux and tails, and was joined onstage by a lovely young black woman who sang backup for the *Gettysburg Address* accompanied by piano. Bob DeWitt, down from Topanga, painted another of his huge, spectacular murals as the show progressed. But what topped it all was the audience: star-studded, including Kirk Douglas, the crowd was voluminous and enthralled. As Charles Tacot suggests, "It was a milestone for class hip concerts. Dick reshaped and restructured the language of the street in his own time, by himself. He saw the potential of that dialogue and brought it into legitimate reality. But at the time, he left many people mystified – they didn't know what the hell he was saying.

"Dick created a format of comedy that took it out of the gin mills and put in into the concert hall. Buckley was different than other comedians – nobody else did four hours of varied, quality humor with characters that made you think.

It was an art form, and he was an artist. But there weren't any concert tours then – not until Peter, Paul & Mary and that crowd – so there was nowhere for Dick to play that kind of show regularly.

"Buckley was a tangent to the world of showbusiness: He was a comic, but he was much more; he was an actor, but not really; he was a writer, but he didn't really write. He didn't have a label – no label fit. Dick was caught in that. He didn't have an identity. He was undefinable. He was alone. But he knew that no one could touch him onstage – he had that artistic immortality."

Buckley's repertoire was extensive and diverse by 1959, including the *Gettysburg* (which he'd written with Mel Welles), *The Nazz*, *The Gasser* – his entire collection of hip translations. If he was in any way nervous or uncomfortable, it didn't show, as he commanded the attention of the multitude and received it with their admiration and esteem. With his powerful, deep voice retelling the numerous translations, he stood tall and erect in the single spotlight, dragging frequently on his cigarette and watching his audience with the look of a commanding officer reviewing his troops. This was the moment he had waited so long for, and he relished every moment.

The rapid-fire bursts were precisely balanced with purposeful pauses, bringing each listener to the edge of their seat, leaning forward to catch the soft, almost sighed words, and then pinning them to their seatbacks with blared declarations of eloquent power. Again, he was in control, pushing the buttons and pulling the strings of an entire audience. And they loved him for it.

The next night was more of the same, with Richard and Laurie seated on stage to watch their father in all his glory. The following night, the 14th, Buckley closed the third and final show to a standing ovation, both deserved and appreciated. Many in that audience were saluting not only His Lordship's brilliant performance of the evening, nor just the years of work that the translations represented, but the more than thirty-five years of showbusiness savvy that was reflected in every glance, every change in inflection or seemingly innocuous gesture, every rhythmic nuance.

Buckley transformed the jazz lingo into poetry of idiom, transcending its street origins and yet remaining faithful to them. More than ever, he fulfilled his dream of theater as a holy experience, and raised entertainment to the pinnacle of art. It was a triumph, pure, plain, and simple. No longer could his critics claim the hip material wouldn't work. No longer could his past hijinks limit his future endeavors.

The future loomed bright and beautiful once more. Or so it seemed.

CHAPTER 8

Mid- '59 was a swingin' time for Lord Buckley.

Richard Bock recorded the *Ivar Concerts*, and with additional material taped a few weeks later he released an album that got off to a fast start, selling several thousand copies within just a few weeks. Illustrated by a series of photos depicting Lord Buckley wearing a pith helmet – shot in front of the *Magic Castle* in Hollywood – *"The Way-Out Humor Of Lord Buckley"* reintroduced His Lordship to those who were already familiar with his more traditional work, and brought him to the attention of thousands more of the Elvis generation for whom the name meant nothing but to whom the material rang with the spirit of Parker and Coltrane, Pollock and Kerouac.

On the straight scene he got a boost when he played the Red Skelton show March 6, and a little over two months later when Ed Sullivan brought him back for another performance. Shot in Alaska, this program featured His Lordship finally performing something other than the four-person pantomime that Ed had demanded seven times during

the preceding decade. In full period costume, Buckley was
filmed in a realistic barroom setting for his dramatic rendition
of *"The Face On The Barroom Floor, or "Dangerous Dan McGroo."*
Buckley filmed two versions of the bit – one hip and one
straight – and Sullivan ultimately decided to run the 'accepted'
standard and so play it safe with his notoriously conservative
longtime viewing audience.

Dressed as a well-heeled stranger, Lord Buckley leaned
against the bar and told the story of Dangerous Dan to an
expectant saloon girl, whose wide eyes reflected the fortunes
of Dan even as His Lordship described them. It was a good
piece, dramatic and meaty, and Buckley carried it off with
practiced aplomb.

In June, Lord Buckley received a very special
invitation, printed on a small white card, from a Dr. Oscar
Janiger of the University of California - Irvine. It invited
Buckley and his family to a July 4th get-together at Lake
Arrowhead, a meeting designed to investigate the properties
of LSD, a powerful hallucinogenic virtually unknown to the -
at-large. His Lordship accepted immediately, and he, Lizbeth,
the kids, and Prince Lewis all drove up into the mountains to
a scenic retreat in the midst of some of the most beautiful
country in the nation. Towering pines, deep clear water,

breathtaking vistas: it was the ideal spot for any vacation, but nearly incomparable as the site for acid experiments.

At the retreat the Buckleys were joined by Jules Buccieri, Thadeus Ashby, Richard Bock, James Coburn, Don Sargent, and several others, most of whom already knew each other. "There was a lot of good power there," Sargent remembers, "a lot of strong energy. Everyone contributed, and the environment was great." Dr. Janiger gathered everyone together on the roof and explained the characteristics of LSD and the expected effects. He went on to describe the testing procedure, which consisted of administering the drug and then interviewing the participants after they'd come down to note their reactions.

What it really amounted to was a giant, organized LSD party with the perfect surroundings and a wild, high-energy group of experimenters. After a day of hiking, water-skiing, and not a little quiet reflection and vivid hallucination, everyone gathered to discuss the day's activities and listen to Don play guitar and sing. Buckley told of his encounter with three nuns while under the influence, and how he charmed them and convinced them he was a maître d´ at a nearby restaurant. In the morning, Lady B. and Mrs. Bouccieri cooked up a hearty breakfast and the procedure repeated itself. After three days of such *scientific* experimentation, Dr. Janiger had the information he sought and Buckley's group of friends had something to compare to their frequent peyote jaunts to Ashby's 'Vanity Fair' cabin on the Lake.

After a quick stop back in Las Vegas, His Lordship returned to L.A. where he'd landed a role as an extra in the film *'Spartacus.'* Richard played a Centurion, complete with toga, shield, and sword, and his presence on the set undoubtedly enlivened the normally boring, repetitive shooting schedule. Two stories, both of which are apocryphal, lend some insight into the image he presented. In the first, a column of Centurions was supposed to march past Kirk Douglas, who was hanging from a cross. Buckley was at the head of the column, and instead of just pausing to look up at Douglas, as was his direction, he supposedly left the group, climbed up on the cross and finally laid over Douglas with his ear near his mouth asking "What? What did you say man?" Douglas is reported to have announced, "I dig a parade," much to the director's dismay.

In the second instance, the Centurions Buckley led were apparently resting between takes, waiting for Laurence Olivier to appear for his shot. Thousands of extras, many of them from U.C.L.A., were also awaiting the star's arrival, and everyone was sweating profusely in the heavy costumes and sweltering heat.

As Olivier finally made his way towards the set, Buckley is said to have jumped up and announced, "Welcome to these shores, Your Grace. I am Lord Buckley, and on behalf of my countrymen, I am honored." Olivier supposedly knew of Buckley's work, as his records were widely-respected in Britain, and stopped to chat for just an instant. Given the opportunity, Lord Buckley launched into *The Pied Piper* translation, and Olivier kept the cast and crew waiting until he finished.

Whether either incident ever occurred or not, it's evident His Lordship was a powerful disruptive force wherever he went. And as co-worker Cecil Rogis remembers, he was certainly flamboyant.

At the wrap party after filming was completed, Lord Buckley showed up wearing his toga and carrying a shield and sword, much to the amazement of all the other cast and crew, who were dressed in street clothes. With an air of total aristocracy, Lord Buckley greeted his friends and leisurely discussed the shooting and other events while constantly eyeballing the huge pile of barbecued chicken that comprised the dinner. Finally, he couldn't resist the chicken any longer, and pulling his sword from its sheath, he attacked the pile with ravenous fury, impaling two pieces on the sword.

Playing the part to its fullest, with the cooperation of several friends, he ordered, "Have the Nigerians bring wine!"

And black friends appeared with wine, bowing and saluting him as "My Lord," as he ate the chicken right from the sword.

With his reputation as a jazz performer growing, Buckley was able to find more gigs in L.A., although still not nearly enough to satisfy his ego or his pocketbook. Harry Bloom and Associates were attempting to manage His Lordship at that time, (as best they could, considering no one could really manage Lord Buckley, with the possible exception of Lady B. on occasion). On October 14, 1959 they were at the *Renaissance* when Buckley delivered a moving thirty-minute eulogy to Errol Flynn. "It was marvelous," Bloom remembers, "spontaneous and touching." Flynn was one of the last of the old-time swashbucklers, a throwback to the days of Barrymore and Fairbanks, and Buckley realized part of him still lived in that era, when daring and graciousness were trademarks of true stars. His Lordship carried that 1930's code of conduct into the 50's and beyond, and Flynn's passing made ever more clear the extreme dichotomy between the two times.

But better days were on the horizon. In addition to his club performances, Bloom arranged for His Lordship to appear on the Jack Parr show, a gig that might very possibly 'break it' for him at last. With the *Ivar* concerts behind him and the *World Pacific* albums off to a quick start, all he needed was the national exposure the *Tonight Show* could offer. So when Bloom brought Lord Buckley out to the Beverly Hilton Hotel to meet the show's associate producer, Buckley was revved and ready to go. "The Lord killed him," says Bloom, and the arrangements were made on the spot for a guest appearance.

But the misfortune that seemed to stalk His Highness appeared once again the night of the show. Mickey Rooney was one of the earlier guests that night, and he appeared on the set drunk and talkative. On and on he rambled, with Paar milking the situation for all it was worth, and then some. Meanwhile, backstage, Buckley saw his allotted time disappearing with every inebriated quip. At last, someone insulted Mickey, or at least he took it as an insult, and off the set he walked. Finally, it was Lord Buckley's turn.

However, it wasn't quite so simple. Originally it had been planned that Lord Buckley come out and chat with Jack for a few minutes before going on to perform *"The Nazz,"* one of his best-known works. With the unexpected loss of time, however, Buckley wasn't called upon to talk with Paar, and his performing slot was so short he had to substitute an abbreviated version of *"The Raven"* for the longer *Nazz*. In his rush to squeeze as much of the translation as possible into the closing moments of the show, His Lordship blew so fast and so furious that only those familiar with the piece could pick up on what he was laying down.

Although he was well-received by the studio audience, to His Highness it was a disaster. His expectations had been so high, and his luck so good, it seemed impossible it could all crumble in just a few minutes with millions of viewers looking on. And what was worse, this time he had played it their way – he had arrived on time, he was fully prepared, and still Fate slapped him away. It was a painful time for His Lordship.

But he persevered.

In a radio interview with KPFA's Bill Butler, Buckley promoted his new *World Pacific* album and explained more about the growth of "the power within," which by then had become an integral element of his life. After relating the story of Álvar Núñez Cabeza de Vaca, *"The Gasser,"* the story of a Spanish officer who in 1510 explored much of the U.S. and discovered *"The Power Within"* ("There is a great power within, that when used in beauty, immaculate conception, and complete purity, can cure and heal and cause miracles to be performed. And when you use it, it spreads like a magic garden, and when you don't use it, it recedes."), His Lordship went on to tell how he had developed his own power to cure. "From this glorious man's adventure, and from the association and the translation of his work, it gave me the power of 'the laying-on of hands,' the healing of the hands, which he said we all have, and I found out that that was true. Each and every one of us possess this."

When Butler asked in semi-amazement if Lord Buckley had ever "proved this," Richard was quick and confident in his reply: "Oh, many times. I've cured arthritis... why, there's a little girl, I ran her down in Las Vegas recently. I heard that she was paralyzed – she went to the hospital with diarrhea and came back paralyzed. I found out where she lived, and she was so nervous that she wouldn't let me put the hand on her. But I explained to her that all over this world, in the alleys, in the valleys, on the plains, on the mesas, on the mountaintops, on the plateaus, through the sand, through the Gulf, through the whole scene of this world – black, blue, green, yellow, and pink, is loaded with beautiful people that we never hear anything about. We only hear about the winners, and the losers, and the others. But they're there, and those people are the protectors and the possessors of the vaults of love, which is known as God. And when you appeal, when you go up a ladder and you go up so that you take your vibrational points spread out so they go round electronic-wise, you contact these people, and you see their beauty, and you hear the voices of the children, you see the sweet swing and the mighty power that's going ahead for greater individual perfection, for greater individual understanding, for greater presentation of the powers of the Garden of Love, and you connect with these people...

"Whapp! You feel a burning right in your hand. I've knocked out arthritis, pain... anything you're big enough to challenge."

To Butler's suggestion that His Lordship's hip semantic reminded him of "the Beat Generation with its jazz language and its Zen Buddhism," Lord Buckley replied: "I've found, in my experience with the Beat Generation, they've turned out to be, in spite of their being maligned and used for publicity purposes and their dark spots pointed out and the white angelic wings of their full beauty ignored, that they're really very strong, and beautiful, and honest and sincere – a Renaissance in youthful Americana. I'm supposed to be a high Sahib of the Beat Generation myself. I've been a beatnik all my life, I guess." Or a true jazzman. As jazzman Sonny Rollins put it, "Jazz has always been a music of integration. In other words, there were definitely lines where blacks would be and where whites would begin to mix a little bit. I mean, jazz was not just a music; it was a social force in this country and it was talking about freedom and people enjoying things for what they are and not having to worry about whether they were supposed to be white, black and all this stuff. Jazz has always been the music that had this kind of spirit."

There were those who thought His Lordship had finally lost it when he spoke of *the power within*, others who thought it was just another of Buckley's many philosophical trial balloons, floated to discover what reaction, if any, he would receive in return. But virtually everyone who came into regular contact with him during 1958-60 has a story to tell about his miraculous cures, and no one who witnessed his efforts doubts his ability to cause at least temporary, and often total recovery from a wide range of ailments. Don Sargent tells of an incident that took place in his shop on Sunset, in which Buckley was visiting when a man came in with a sick child who had a severe cough. Buckley, always ready to converse with a child under any circumstances, asked the little boy how long he had had the cough, and to the reply "a long time" he put his hands on the child's chest and told the boy "I'm going to give you a lot of energy. Feel better baby, feel good." According to Sargent, the boy was better within a couple of days. And on another occasion a man who'd been in an auto accident was complaining of constant headaches until Buckley put his hands on the man and softly reassured him that he'd be okay. The pain disappeared.

With Lord Buckley's expanding consciousness came a realization that certain environmental factors he'd come to accept as inevitable were, in fact, negative life influences.

Despite the southern California mania for sunshine, and his own longtime love for the golden rays, Lord Buckley came to the conclusion that extensive tanning caused cancer and aggravated other diseases. "Like with the Indians," Robert Mitchum remembers Buckley saying, "it wasn't the cowboys that got 'em, it was the sun." In the same vein, when Richard Bock introduced him to a vegetarian diet, he did his best to follow its strict eating limitations, and for a while ate little other than fruits, nuts, and vegetables. Until the Paar debacle, his drinking even subsided.

"He was a visionary," Mitchum explains, "and very logical except where *he* was concerned. A total iconoclast, the only thing precious to him was life, people – he had a great sense of joy."

One of his many stories proclaimed this joy as a religious experience, and captured his love for humanity most explicitly. "Very recently on the San Bernardino Freeway," he'd begin softly, "I got hung up in an old junker car going to Las Vegas, Nevada. Right in the middle of the freeway, during the rush hour, it conked out. It was a madhouse, like having lunch in the middle of the Indianapolis Speedway.

About three days went by and finally along came God. There was two of 'em: a big God and a little God. They didn't know me, but they pushed and they pulled, and they twisted and they yanked, and they gave me every possible assistance in the world. And they finally got me on my way. I haven't seen 'em since. I think that people – I hope I haven't offended your religious beliefs – but I think that people should worship people. I really do."

For most of 1959, Lord Buckley tried to make his mark in and around Los Angeles, and although he worked fairly steadily, there was no breakthrough to cheer him on, only the ghosts of 'might have been' to remind him of his past. A gig as the voice of "Go Man Van Gogh" on the *Beanie and Cecil* cartoon show gave him the opportunity to spread the hip word to youngsters and gain some further national publicity, but the character was short-lived and it was only his voice that gained widespread new attention, not his own image and act.

As Los Angeles faded as the city of opportunity, Lord Buckley turned his sights northward, to the San Francisco area. His Lordship had begun his professional career in the Bay area over thirty years earlier, and occasional return visits – most notably in the mid-forties – had been well-received by the locals. Also, San Francisco was well known as one of the hipper and more sophisticated American cities, and prejudices against new ideas or lifestyles were relatively non-existent.

Lord Buckley and Prince Lewis returned briefly to Las Vegas, where they packed up the Buckley household and crammed the entire family into the Olds for the journey to Sausalito. There, a friend of His Lordship's who was connected with the Kingston Trio found them a place to stay: "a hideaway pad on a wharf that looked like it was in the middle of a junkyard." The squat, concrete house looked like a military bunker from the outside, but inside was decorated comfortably, and was large enough to house the entire family as well as six or seven other 'beatnik types' who slept in hammocks or on the floor.

San Francisco was just experiencing a boom in club entertainment, with the Smothers Brothers, the Christy Minstrels, and the Kingston Trio, among others, all very big. Lord Buckley's style of performing was, of course, considerably different than that of the young up-and-comers, encompassing a combination of techniques and influences from Shakespearean drama to hipster and beat. The last two represented the latest evolution and refinement of bohemian culture, with the distinction obscure to all but the most inside of insiders.

Despite the difference, or perhaps because of it, Buckley was still able to land gigs throughout the area, though often working only weekends making just enough to get by. At one such booking, a Monday-nights-only gig at the *Coffee Gallery* in North Beach, Buckley played two shows nightly for five weeks, drawing packed houses for each set. His Lordship performed from behind a lectern in the small, crowded coffeehouse, dressing casually (for him) and often sporting a snappy hat with a small feather in the band. His reception was enthusiastic, as the crowd was San Francisco's cream of the beatnik set. Throughout the month, he regaled audiences with dozens of hip bits as well as constant, sharp improvisation and philosophical asides that probed subjects rarely discussed in public arenas, from UFO's to an assortment of belief systems.

But not everyone was able to relate to Lord Buckley's style and point of view. One night at the *Gallery*, while His Highness was presenting a piece that involved a black dialect, a young man stood up and called him a Nazi, accusing him of prejudice against blacks. Lord Buckley was stunned. For decades before most whites had even thought about the black plight, Buckley had been not only a defender of black rights, but a friend of any person "black, white, red, yellow, pink or blue." His black characters were no more singled-out than any of 35 others, and all were integral components of his act

– and himself. After the heckler left, Buckley spent just a few seconds excusing the interruption and then continued with the show. But the words hurt, and it emphasized to His Lordship how far removed from some of the young radicals he was, even though by all rights, he should've been their patron saint.

Buckley worked throughout the Bay area: in Berkeley at the *"Old Towne Coffeehouse"* in Sausalito, at the *"hungry i"* in San Francisco, even at a small organic restaurant in Mill Valley. He recorded a series of new bits, including *"His Majesty the Pedestrian"* and *"H.M. The Policeman,"* in a small studio just around the block from the wharf, and met Lawrence Ferlinghetti, the high priest of beat literature, who agreed to publish a collection of several Buckley translations. With so much happening, it seemed the move north had been the right decision, and the Buckleys sought a permanent house where they could establish a real home.

According to legend, one afternoon Lord Buckley saw a large house being moved and inquired if it were available. He was told the owner had been trying to sell the place, and was now moving it to San Raphael where he would be interested in any proposition whatsoever. Somehow, with virtually no money, His Highness managed to persuade the owner to let the family move in, and so in March of 1959 they did. The house, at 188 Prospect St., was located at the edge of town, up on a large hill. A stream ran through the property, and it was surrounded by all sorts of greenery, trees, and flowers. A large, two-story home, it had incurred some damage in the move (a large poster covered a deep crack in the wall), but was still a beautiful old place with lots of room and a "good feeling" about it that everyone who visited remarked upon. Madame Daganova, Lady B's ballet instructor, came out from New York for an Imperial visit, as did Richard's sister, Nell. New friends from the surrounding area, as well as old showbiz associates such as tap-dancer Tommy Conine, stopped by for the kind of old-style partying that His Lordship was known-for coast to coast.

When large groups appeared, there was always plenty of room at the dinner table, a long, narrow banquet table that sat twelve. The children would pick huge leaves from the trees on the property and use them as placemats, and Lizbeth would work her magic to sort, arrange, and feed   virtually any number of people with whatever resources were available. Once again, for the umpteenth time, fortune seemed to give Lord Buckley the high sign, and San Raphael became the locale for a swingin' new Royal Court – a bit more mellow, but still unique and highly imaginative.

A mutual friend introduced Buckley to Michael DuPont, the owner of *'Outside at the Inside'* in Palo Alto, and before long Buckley was booked at the classy hip club and creating a new following from local students, beatniks, and lucky accidental viewers. The club was distinctive for its removable roof, marble tables, suspended space heaters, and top jazz musicians, but two factors made it even more

unusual: a dress code was strictly enforced, and because of its proximity to a college, there was no alcohol. Nonetheless, the place was almost always jumping, and Buckley fit right in.

A few people were upset with Buckley's act, calling *"The Nazz"* sacrilegious, and many others were unable to pick up on the fast-paced hip talk, but most appreciated His Lordship for his presence and captivating energy and he was well-received by customers and critics alike. In an April 16 *San Francisco Chronicle* entertainment column, Buckley received a glowing mini-review that touted his future success: "The leader of the cool cats, Lord Buckley, continues to hold sway over the weekend crowds at Palo Alto's 'Outside at the Inside.' With two albums of his way-out humor to his credit, this hip-talking genius is building a following of national importance."

At that point Buckley, had been playing weekends at the club for over three months, with such jazz notables as singer Jo Ryder and the Mary Hubbard Trio included on the bill. While performing at one of his other coffeehouse dates, Buckley met a young performer by the name of Del Close, who became a director at Second City in Chicago. Close remembers His Highness was "wearing a tux that was too short, army boots, spats, with the legs of his trousers rolled up. For the first time I realized he was white."

Lord Buckley tried out some new material, which didn't click, and went into a 25-minute version of *The Pied Piper* that lost all but his most loyal followers by its conclusion. In a conversation after his appearance, Richard solicited Del's reactions and evaluation, and was somewhat surprised to hear that Close thought he'd pushed the audience too far and hadn't condensed his material sufficiently.

Far from being upset, however, Buckley listened intently, and the two men hit it off well enough to propose playing a concert together in June. But in the meantime, Buckley's career was rattled by a string of setbacks that shattered his plans for a San Francisco comeback. First, on May 22, *"Hiparama"* was released. His Lordship had high expectations for this print collection of hip classics, especially since he was working with Mr. Ferlinghetti, whose star was in ascendence among hip performers and intellectuals nationwide. However, the collaboration never gained momentum, and the book sold disappointingly. Buckley was surprised, but hoped sales would pick up with increased bookings of the hip material in live shows.

It was on that count he suffered his second setback. The *'hungry i'* was one of Frisco's most notable nightclubs during the early 60's, and a long run at the *'i'* meant considerable exposure and national attention. Through a friend, Charles Campbell, Buckley got a short gig at the club, and was successful enough to earn a tentative promise for a longer date later on. As fate would have it, the next act booked into the *'i'* was a young comedian by the name of Mort Sahl, who became a regular fixture at the club for the next three years.

And finally, there was the big concert with Del Close. A producer friend had booked a hot local jazz band and a tap dancer to appear with Lord Buckley and Del, and rented a good-sized auditorium in Concord, CA. Prince Lewis had traded in his Olds on a new, red Volkswagen mini-bus, complete with an American flag hanging from the antenna, and on the afternoon of June 26 Buckley, Close, and Lewis all drove around Concord in the *Fairyland Express #2* trying to generate interest in the concert scheduled for that night. What they hadn't realized when they booked the show, however, was that the Patterson-Johannsen heavyweight championship fight was also scheduled the same night, and when Buckley & Co. arrived at the auditorium they found only a handful of spectators awaiting them. But Lord Buckley was not one to back-out on a performance, and so the show went on as scheduled, with His Highness contributing over two hours to his small but appreciative audience. In a conversation immediately after the show, the producer suggested to Buckley they might have drawn more people if they'd played in San Francisco instead of the boonies. "We could've drawn more people if we'd played on the moon," His Lordship sniped disgustedly, and even as they drove home a new plan was formulating in Buckley's mind, spurred on by Del's invitation to come out to Chicago – where they could do it right.

CHAPTER 9

After two months of preparation and consideration, Lord Buckley had a plan. He'd play a few final West Coast shows, then tie-in a *Second City* performance with a nearby Cincinnati gig, before continuing on to New York, where, according to Redd Foxx, who saw him in San Francisco just before he left, "he was going to The City for a fight." A fight for artistic, philosophic, and financial survival.

A strong political awareness was taking root in Lord Buckley's consciousness, inspired by the candidacy of John F. Kennedy, with its emphasis on personal action and its vision of a hopeful, people-oriented New Frontier. Buckley and his friends watched the campaign on television and frequently debated the various platforms and personalities, with Lord Buckley a steadfast Kennedy supporter.

In August, at the *Renaissance Club* in L.A., Lord Buckley joined Del Close for "his final appearance on the West Coast prior to *The Cosmic Tour*," and then said his goodbyes, sent the family back to Las Vegas, and caught a plane for Cincinnati. He'd invited his son, Fred, then 23, to join him on Tour so

His Lordship could show him the ropes of showbiz, but Fred was caught-up in the summer water sports of Bullhead City and declined. Prince Lewis followed in the mini-bus, arriving several days later to find His Lordship surrounded by friends and living quite comfortably. He appeared at the *Prophet Coffee House* and the *Rivoli Burlesque Theater*, and became an instant street celebrity by driving through city streets standing up in the VW, with his head and shoulders sticking out of the sunroof, directing Lewis at the top of his lungs:

"Forward!... Left!... Right!" he'd bellow, and Lewis would respond accordingly.

Lord Buckley did some recording at the home of Bob Gray, a musician friend, and attended a flurry of parties – both in his honor and with friends. The shows went well, and the entire stay in Cincinnati was a pleasant beginning for his tour. But, as always, soon it was time to move on – this time to Chicago for the impending concert with Del Close.

In celebration of his long-awaited return to the Windy City, Del, Ted Travers, and others arranged for a spectacular party to welcome His Highness back. As the Fairyland Express worked its way through the crowded city streets in late afternoon, however, it appeared for a moment the party might have to be delayed. "I think we're lost," Lewis informed Lord Buckley as they tried to circumvent heavy traffic. "Drive on, Prince," Buckley intoned, "every street is a beautiful street."

Finally, at 4 p.m., the Mini-bus pulled up in front of a beer garden situated next door to *Second City*, and the festivities began. A red carpet was unfurled, minstrels played, and many of the two dozen guests knelt and kissed His Lordship's hand in greeting.

Buckley was seated on a throne of honor, and expounded on His philosophies while serving girls tread on empty speed capsules while bringing him his drinks. With such an auspicious beginning, it was a bit of a bring-down to find the room he was to stay in was "a creepy little apartment around the corner from *Second City*." When Barbara Harris and Del visited Buckley, they were appalled by the cockroaches that overran the apartment and asked Lewis why they didn't spray them. "Not without dropping leaflets first," Lord Buckley interjected as he walked into the room, and so the small but numerous inhabitants were saved. It took another friend, Rex Benson, to save Lewis and His Lordship from their dreadful living quarters, as he got them a trade-out at the Maryland Hotel – where they moved directly.

Benson, a fellow comic, tried to get Buckley work in an assortment of potentially lucrative deals, but none of them ever quite clicked. A gig with His Lordship reporting the news hip-style was arranged for $50/week, but after just a few presentations the project folded. And a Coca-Cola ad exec was convinced that Lord Buckley could represent the company with just the right dignified hipness to really move some Coke, but the morning of a 10 a.m. meeting to discuss the details, Buckley showed up over an hour late with two gaudy young ladies clinging to his arms. Needless to say, he wasn't hired.

News from New York was quite hopeful, however. Harold Humes, a novelist and Buckley enthusiast, arranged for an extended appearance at a hip jazz club, and Mort Fagua, a d.j., was helping publicize the upcoming event by playing His Lordship's records. The timing – with his opening scheduled for early October – fit in well with The Tour and guaranteed enough money to get something good going in New York. Lord Buckley wasn't sure what direction his life should take, but a gut instinct told him New York was the place to confront his future, and his past, and settle once and for all his lifelong duel with destiny.

But first came his commitments in Chicago, his old hometown and the scene of some of his greatest triumphs. Yet it had been years since he'd played there, and the only time he'd tried his hip material, it had bombed. Still, he knew a large clique of loyal fans would turn out for this special show, and his reception had rekindled the confidence that had moved thousands thirty years earlier in the Walkathons.

Del Close enlisted Severin Dardin to join Buckley and him in the show, entitled *'Seacoast of Bohemia,'* and spread the word it was going to be something truly exceptional. For one thing, there were three comedians carrying the entire show. And of course, one of them was Lord Buckley. On a Monday night, 180 people crowded into the club well before showtime, and others pushed their way in to stand in the back.

As Dell recalls: "It was a memorable evening. All these people had been listening to mother-in-law jokes for years, and then here was something that really mattered." For Lord Buckley, it was a transcendent night that encapsulated his 35 years in the business into a brilliant two-hour set. From a classic four-person pantomime featuring an alderman and a black hooker as the two love-struck members of the group, to his hip translations, complex stories, and sizzling ad-libs, he captivated and entranced the audience, creating new worlds that graphically illustrated his real-world philosophies.

Buckley swept them away with his eloquence, energy, and elocution, and then snapped them back to reality with a new outlook that many among them had never even considered.

Buckley's magic did not go unnoticed. Alan Ribback, the owner of the *Gate of Horn*, hired His Lordship to do a series of late-night shows at his club, and Buckley gladly signed on. Appearing at the *Gate* during the early hours were Hamilton Camp and Bob Gibson, a young folk-singing duo who were just building a following in the Chicago area. "When Buckley walked in," Camp recalls, "he'd greet everyone with something like 'Good evening, Your Grace.' He made us all feel like somebody." He gave everyone he met standing and walking lessons, and at one time had six people following him around in a parade as they practiced their posture and carriage.

To promote his gig, Lord Buckley made himself available for interviews and any other coverage he could muster, hoping to turn the *Gate* appearances into a Chicago comeback. Most notable of those efforts was an interview with noted WFMT radio personality Studs Terkel, whose exposure to His Highness left a definite impression.

Terkel compared recordings of His Lordship's translations of Antony's funeral oration, *The Pied Piper,* and *The Raven* with straight versions by Marlon Brando, Boris Karloff, and Basil Rathbone, respectively. Not only were the contrasts striking, but most impressively, Buckley held his

own with each of the 'legitimate' masters, giving new vibrance
and expanded meaning to the classic tales.

His Lordship set the tone with his opening greeting:
"To all the swingers, and all the goers, and all the divinities of
the high rhythm of the sweet jump of the flash of the sound
of life itself into the language of the people, all the swingers
on this royal FM, may I say - BELOVED."

Explaining the development of his hip material,
Buckley revealed," I've been interested in doing these hip
semantics for quite some time. Primarily I became interested
in them because of the tremendous advantage you have with
the youth of the nation. The hip talk seems to be more or less
their language, and in translating the great classics of our
time, I thought it would be a splendid way to bring the
beautiful sounds to their attention. A high school teacher tells
me they've been using my translation of *'Friends, Romans &
Countrymen'* to explain to the children exactly what
Shakespeare said."

Between high-pitched giggles as His Lordship related
some of the background details surrounding Caesar's death,
Terkel explained to his listeners, "half of it is watching Lord
Buckley in action. I think it is imperative that people, to fully
appreciate His Highness, Lord Buckley, His Hipness, see him
as well. Because in the doing of it there's a physicalization.

Your Highness, you have the mark of an old-time
Shakespearean actor... and yet the tempo you have is that of a
jazz tempo... It has the flexibility, the excitement, the beat and
the blues feeling."

Buckley agreed with Studs' interpretation, and added
his sentiments about working with such timeless pieces for
his translations.

"When you start to fool with these classics, you have
the tremulous stature of an amateur architect goofing in the
Taj Mahal: 'There must be *something* I can do here...' So it's
fairly dangerous work to begin with."

Touching on the religious aspects of many of His
Lordship's works, Terkel pointed out that while some people
thought *The Nazz* was sacrilegious, most found it to be "a
highly devout interpretation."

"Well, in the three miracles I have on our Savior, from
the life of Jesus," Buckley explained, "preachers tell me
they're bringing hot-rodders into the Church with them...
Unquestionably and positively *(The Nazz)* is a religious psalm.
I'm not a sick humorist. I admire all kinds of humor, and all
of it's necessary – evidently there wouldn't be sick humor if
there weren't sick people."

In closing, His Lordship brought his generalized
beliefs to bear on a specific problem in Chicago: gangs. "To
all the solid cats and kitties that swing this precious cherry

land of America, may you always put it down solid, and in great truth, and in great beauty. And it is the prayer of the hipsters that the gangs – the Cobras, and all the gangs – quit squaring up and get hip, which means to be wise, and make the people who love them proud of them."

Shorn of all humor and spoken with great sincerity, Buckley's words moved Studs and undoubtedly most everyone who heard the broadcast. But once His Lordship was back on the streets, the necessities of self-promotion and daily entertainment took precedence over his philosophical bent, and His Highness travelled throughout the city fulfilling his personal and professional wants and needs.

One afternoon, Prince Lewis and Lord Buckley drove out to the Chicago Bears summer camp in Rensselaer, Indiana, where His Lordship was to meet with the players and stage an informal performance. On the way out of the city, the Ferryland Express passed a long line of cars that had overheated. Buckley, feeling sassy, leaned out of the VW as they whizzed by and yelled, "I told you to bring a picnic lunch!" The show at the Bears camp went beautifully, but only because the drivers of those broken-down cars couldn't catch the VW on foot – though a few tried.

Visiting his old friend Jack Green a few days later, Lord Buckley and Lewis were met at the door by Jack's daughter, Karen, resplendent in a Roman toga and laurel wreath for a Latin Club function. Neither man even mentioned her strange attire, but when it came up in the conversation that they hadn't yet eaten dinner, they were invited to stay and managed to devour "about twenty" lamb chops in a twinkling.

Later that night, Karen was awakened by an inebriated Lord Buckley who explained to her, "No matter where you travel throughout your life, the only word you'll ever have to remember is etcetera." Satisfied with his pronouncement, His Lordship left, and after a few confused moments, Karen fell back to sleep.

As was often the case, His Highness spent many of his after-hours at his favorite clubs, where he would hold Court with a small group of friends – new and old. At one such gathering, Buckley noticed an attractive woman staring at the goings-on with undisguised fascination, and he invited her to join them. Princess Bunny, as she was immediately dubbed, was included in his travelling Court as of their first meeting. When they left that night, Bunny was part of Cosmic Tour Buckley. Lewis, Bunny, an executive of the Gas company, another stripper, and the violin player from the club band – all climbed into the VW mini-bus and drove down Rush St. in the wee hours of the morning with the violin player wailing away on his instrument.

To awaken the younger generation to His Lordship's *Gate of Horn* appearance, Buckley & Co. made their way out to the University of Chicago, where they dropped in to a 'liberal' fraternity at which a black consciousness group was performing an ad-libbed tribal dance, complete with traditional music and costumes. With such a gathering of young people all primed for entertainment, His Highness informed the hostess he would be willing to perform a few bits for the crowd if she so desired. The young woman wouldn't hear of imposing on such a regal character, and so politely insisted Buckley and his friends just relax and enjoy themselves. Of course, for His Lordship that was just the invitation he needed, since performing was how he enjoyed himself. And since the party was black-oriented, he immediately launched into some Amos and Andy characters.

"Everyone was askance," according to Del Close, but Buckley would no more hesitate to do his favorite impressions for blacks than for any other group, and he plowed on. A polite but decidedly cool reception and the urgings of his friends ended the performance, but Lord Buckley was neither ashamed nor embarrassed, except for the youngsters who couldn't comprehend that his humor was based in love and dedicated as a tribute.

All his efforts at hyping the *Gate* gig apparently paid off, for not only were his early a.m. shows well-attended (1 a.m. on weekdays, 2:30 a.m. on weekends). But the BBC chose his appearance there to tape a documentary about one of Britain's more popular comedians: Lord Buckley. The night of the BBC taping, His Lordship was three-fourths of the way through his act when he suddenly became too ill to continue and walked unsteadily offstage. Later, Hamilton Camp saw him slumped over in the back of the BBC bus, his face ashen.

Apparently, His Lordship had suffered a 'baby stroke', but in a short while the physical effects of the stroke disappeared and so he returned to his usual schedule. However, in retrospect it seems likely that Buckley suffered more than his visible symptoms, as his behavior over the next few weeks pointed to lingering effects.

"After the stroke he did some things that terrified audiences," Severin Dardin recalls, "including a bit about this couple in a blue boat on a black lake. A mean cat met them, and it was gruesome – they were destroyed. It was really scary. One time when he was telling it, a young couple tried to walk out and he forbade them to leave. So they sat back down, cowering."

Severin found himself on the receiving end of this dark side of Buckley a few weeks later. He and Lord Buckley had

been good friends since the *Seacoast* gig, and in fact, His
Highness had laid hands on Dardin at one point to cure a
headache. But one night after a show, Buckley came suddenly
unglued and punched Severin in the stomach with no
apparent reason. "He was clearly in the advanced stages of
some disease," Del Close suggests. "He showed outbursts of
rage, sudden stoppages in his performances – he was certainly
sick."

Yet outwardly, His Lordship seemed to be as hearty as
ever, and since his flareups were infrequent, most of his
friends never realized anything was amiss. But a phone call to
his old buddy Bob DeWitt in California suggested all was not
well. "The Lord called me long distance from Chicago,"
DeWitt remembered. "I thought he was in need of money, as
I had sent him money in the past when he called me, but this
time he said, "You've got to come here and join me in
Chicago. I'm playing the *Gate of Horn* and I'm calling you
from the 1-2-3 story ring-a-ding building and the owner of
the building and the club is on the other end of this
telephone conversation and he says I don't have any true
friends. So come and do a program with me onstage at the
Gate of Horn. I will have a car at the airport for you, and lots
of girls to take care of you while you are here.' Then he said,

'you need to come and get off the West Coast as you have
been there too long and I love you.'"

DeWitt couldn't be persuaded to leave his family in
Topanga, but he told his Lordship, "you can tell the leader of
the 123 story ring-a-ding building in Chicago that you do
have a true friend, Bob DeWitt, who stands at the Church of
the Living Swing in Topanga, always open for the Lord's
return – our leader and lightning rod.

"And I hung up on the Lord, with him still pleading
with me to come and join him."

As September faded into October, the Chicago gig was
over and it was time to pack up the mobile Royal Court once
more for the final leg of the *"Cosmic Tour."* With a small group
of friends to bid them adieu, His Lordship, Prince Lewis, and
Lady Bunny climbed into the Ferryland Express #2 and
began the long trip East.

CHAPTER 10

Buckley was sky-high for the trip back to New York. The opportunity to return to the Big Apple meant more than just a well-paying gig, (he was promised $450/week), more even than seeing a multitude of old friends.

New York was the *BIGTIME*, the one and only. From the earliest days of his career, it had been the ultimate destination for every entertainer in the biz, aspiring or successful, and certainly Buckley knew show biz as well as anyone around.

Riding in the VW microbus, with Prince Lewis manning the wheel at speeds that frequently exceeded accepted limits, His Lordship talked fervently about the future with the zest of a born-again performer. The Fairyland Express screeched into New York on Oct. 4th, depositing Buckley, Lady Bunny, and Prince Lewis at a fairly luxurious rented apartment at 39 Gramercy Park: $500 a month bought quite a bit in 1960.

No sooner did Richard set up residence, than the usual assortment of friends and potential friends began appearing at his doorstep. Druggies, musicians, hookers, writers,

performers – they were all there. An agent friend promised
him women; others brought booze and an assortment of
drugs. But most of his visitors just brought themselves, to be
entertained, to be excited, and to party.

At first, everything went smoothly. With Humes
directing his professional life, and Bunny and Lewis helping
as best they could to organize his chaotic social life, Richard
made headway in the confused arena of New York politics
and entertainment. One of the first hurdles to overcome was
the acquisition of a controversial 'cabaret card.' Until 1941,
cabarets and other small clubs that served liquor were
licensed by the City Department of Licenses. But then,
responding to the widely-held belief that "nightclubs owned
or controlled by gangsters were used as regular meeting
placed of criminals," cabaret licensing was made the province
of the Police Department.

Every employee of every cabaret was required to
submit him- or herself to fingerprinting, mugshots, and a $2
fee. Without the card, you didn't work. Or so the statute read.

In practice, however, the law was used discriminately
at the discretion of the police. Sophie Tucker worked without
one; Frank Sinatra publicity admitted not even having applied
when he worked at the Copa; and even the American Guild

of Variety Artists President Joey Adams appeared without the card.

It was an extremely unpopular law, but nonetheless it was still the law. So Buckley and Humes filled out the required paperwork, posed dutifully for photographs, and paid the token fee to receive a temporary permit that served until the actual document was processed.

In good spirits and feeling fully recovered from his attack in Chicago, Richard was more than ready to get back to work. *The Jazz Gallery*, once a modestly popular hang-out for the hip crowd, was experiencing some hard times and hoped the return of an old favorite might help them get back on track. Humes' enthusiastic endorsements had convinced them Buckley might just be the man to pump some energy into the club.

However, despite advertisements on the radio and in the papers, even some of His Highness's old friends did not know he was in town until he was gone. The word spread slowly, moving first through the artists and intelligentsia, then to the hipcats.

So no one was quite sure what was going to happen when Buckley took the stage that first night. But it is doubtful he was too surprised when he saw a good but not capacity audience awaiting him. Bolstered and directed by some of his old friends and admirers, the audience was responsive as he ran through a sizeable portion of his hip repertoire: everything from *The Nazz* to *The Pedestrian.*

Constantly puffing on a cigarette, Buckley changed dialects like other performers changed hats. One minute he was a hip cat blowin' some riffs, and the next a tottering old man, or a southern Negro. He was solid all the way.

A strong ovation enheartened him as he left the stage, but the lack of a full house at his opening night nagged at the back of his mind and ego. He had hoped for better. His travelling troupe of friends and admirers helped soothe the pain with their compliments, and a long night of partying helped Richard justify the disappointment of unfulfilled expectations.

For twelve days the routine continued: off to the club, at 80 St. Marks Place, arriving by 10; two one-hour shows, and then off into the wilds of Manhattan for three, ten, even twenty hours of revelry. Most of the time the party was at his place. He felt comfortable there – everyone knew where he was, and he was in charge. Some nights, between, before, or during festivities, Buckley and Prince Lewis set off in the VW bus to search out new worlds, to go where nobody ever thought of going or ever wanted to go. Uptown, downtown, to the ends of the island and beyond. Racing through the streets during the early hours of the morning, His Highness directed Lewis with casual indifference as he entertained him with stories, plans, thoughts, and new pieces of business.

Buckley loved to get lost, to see what was around the next corner or across the way. His enthusiasm for the adventure of a trip was matched only by the joy he felt at pretending to total strangers that he was, say, "Dr. Ridley," on an emergency mission that required immediate directions.

Late one night, cruising back toward the apartment down Fifth Avenue, His Highness directed Lewis to drive continuously onward, regardless of the color of the innumerable traffic lights. For miles they drove through the nearly silent canyons of New York, whizzing through intersections with the audacity of a police car in hot pursuit. If any fingers were crossed, they certainly weren't Buckley's. He refused to listen to less intrepid suggestions, and forged onward with a bravado reflected in his words of encouragement and in his ever-changing pose: either hanging out the window or standing erect with his head sticking up out of the sunroof. Occasionally he hailed the lonely pedestrians, shouting whatever words of advice he might decide upon at the spur of the moment. Or, more likely, scaring the hell out of them with his piercingly accurate train whistle impression.

Arriving, at last, back at the apartment, Lewis dropped
His Lordship at the front door and drove around the corner
to park the minibus. No sooner did Buckley disappear into
the building, however, than a police cruiser pulled up behind
Lewis with its flashers blinking.

This sort of existence went on until October 20th,
with Lord Buckley visiting and relaxing during the day,
partying at night after the show. A couple of times he even
went to record stores to promote his albums and
"Hiparama." But the turnouts were small, and the bookings
not terribly successful. His audiences at the club were
enthusiastic, but not large. In fact, the owners of the Gallery
suggested a pay-cut, at least temporarily. Buckley refused.

On the night of the 20th, Richard was racing through a
routine at the *Gallery*, unmindful of the police officers who
had entered up front. Without warning, the unwilling owner
suddenly walked on stage and stopped His Lordship's
performance. The crowd jeered, without effect. At a loss for
words for one of the few times in his career, Buckley left
quietly.

The Police Department had decided to revoke
Richard's temporary cabaret card, citing an erroneous answer
to a question on the application that demanded whether the
applicant had ever been "arrested or summoned" for any

offense other than a traffic violation. An FBI check turned up three arrests: the first, in 1941 in Reno (for being drunk); the second, in 1943 in Indianapolis (charge dropped); and lastly in 1946 for assault and possession of marijuana (no disposition.)

Buckley, when confronted by the charges, said he had misunderstood the application – he thought they meant criminal convictions, since arrests meant nothing more than police supposition, and drunkenness was hardly a crime.

The boys in blue were not convinced. Without his card, Lord Buckley was unemployable in any establishment that served liquor. And for an entertainer like Buckley, that meant he was out of work. Richard hired well-regarded NY lawyer Maxwell Cohen to represent him, and searched out every possible lead toward getting his card back again. One such lead took him to the Park Sheraton Hotel on October 24th.

According to Lord Buckley's manager, Harold Humes, a Broadway theatrical agent by the name of Phil Kepness had been told by a 'Mr. Winters' that "Buckley could get his card to go back to work... for $100. Winters said it was a deputy police commissioner he was seeing. He met with the deputy and Buckley in an East Side hotel, the Sheraton-something.

Winters introduced the deputy police commissioner and the commissioner invited Buckley to the affair that night."

"The affair" in question was a benefit for the Police Honor Legion, held October 24th at the *Park Sheraton Hotel*. Buckley performed free, receiving only a meal and some appreciative applause for his efforts. Two days later, a hearing was held at the Police Department's Division of Licenses, at which Buckley and Max Cohen argued that the revocation of Lord Buckley's cabaret card not only deprived him of his livelihood, but was carried out in violation of the Department's own regulations.

"You are not allowed to 'revoke or suspend' even temporary cards until the card-holder has received 'notice and hearing'," Cohen stated, quoting in part from the regulations themselves.

After listening to Cohen's arguments, Deputy Chief Inspector Frank W. Lent, who was presiding at the hearing, insisted the police had not transgressed procedures and abruptly adjourned the case without immediately setting a date for resumption. However, he did indicate "that he was considering the possibility of issuing a temporary cabaret card to Buckley pending the outcome of the case."

That sounded wonderful to Lord Buckley. "Maybe I can entertain the police again," he said. "I enjoyed performing

for them the other night. I really love the Police department.
What would we do without the police?"

Despite his optimism, Lord Buckley would never again
perform on stage.

For two weeks Buckley awaited news from Cohen
regarding the proposed temporary card, or at least a new date
for a resumption of the hearing. Finally, he learned the case
would be discussed on the following Monday, November 14.

His Lordship passed the time drinking beer, smoking,
and talking with friends, deeply concerned yet unwilling to let
the tide of events sweep him off the street. He looked tired
and drawn, less "buoyant and saucy" than his normal self. But
people still came to laugh and be entertained – and Buckley
couldn't say no.

Hopeful that some of his more prominent friends
might stop by and offer sage advice (and perhaps a small
loan), he scanned the papers looking for openings and
advertisements. One day, when he learned that Anthony
Quinn was appearing in *"Becket"* on Broadway, he dispatched
Lewis to bring Quinn his regards. Quinn received the
messenger, but begged off, saying he hoped to make it at a
later date. Buckley was disappointed.

On the night of November 11, he was visited by a
"strange, hostile group" of people who apparently dabbled in

voodoo and the occult. Buckley received them as he did everyone who sought him out, and for a time they talked and sipped wine. But something disturbed Richard, and in a fit of pique he asked them to leave.

Most unusual. Lord Buckley almost never asked a guest to leave the party; he refused to let the situation get that far out of control. But he wouldn't discuss the incident any more fully than the bare details, and went to bed that night in a dark mood. The next morning, Buckley wasn't up at his usual hour. When Prince Lewis went to investigate, he found His Lordship partially paralyzed, his right side nearly totally deadened. In Buckley's words, "the bug-bird's in me." Though Lewis wanted to call the hospital, Richard refused. He had always felt that hospitals killed people, and was not about to let them get their hands on him unless it was absolutely necessary. By five o'clock in the afternoon, it was necessary: Buckley had slipped into a coma.

A short time later, confused and panicky, Prince Lewis called longtime Buckley friend Ed Sullivan for advice. Sullivan directed Lewis to call a hospital immediately, and then to contact Lady Buckley in Las Vegas.

An ambulance rushed Buckley to nearby Columbus Hospital, where Lewis and Lady Bunny waited anxiously for word of his condition. Barred from his room (family only), they paced the hallway as the hours passed. Near 8 o'clock, unable to restrain herself any longer, Bunny slipped into the room when no one was looking and took up a vigil at his bedside.

In Las Vegas, Lizbeth had made immediate reservations to fly to New York, and was repeatedly on the phone trying to speak to her beloved husband, asking to "Please put the phone up to his ear and let me talk to him."

But Buckley's condition worsened, and he remained unconscious. Caressing his hand with her own, Lady Bunny peered desperately into a face not yet ready to die. He didn't move, his eyes closed to the world.

A short time later, with Bunny still clutching his hand, Lord Richard Buckley set off on what was to be his final Cosmic Tour.

It was November 12, 1960, and he was 54.

EPILOGUE

The reaction to Buckley's death was instantaneous and explosive.

A distinguished group of writers, editors, musicians, and performers (including Humes, Norman Mailer, Theodore Bikel, and Nat Hentoff) banded together as the Citizens Emergency Committee to protest "police harassment" in the Buckley case, and to challenge the very existence of cabaret licensing.

Front page headlines reported an emotional Bureau of Licenses hearing Monday, November 14th; Humes, Cohen and others charged that the system of licensing cabaret entertainers had "led to widespread police corruption."

Deputy commissioner Edward McCabe, Deputy Commissioner Leonard Reisman, Deputy Chief Inspector Lent, and even Police Commissioner Stephen P. Kennedy attended the hearing, which quickly developed into a heated exchange "that could be heard through all five floors of the building at the corner of Worth and Greenwich streets."

When Kennedy turned on one member of the Committee and began shouting questions ("Who are the '*citizens*'?" "What is the *emergency*?" "Were you ever known by any other name?"), Maxwell Cohen exploded.

"That was a stupid question," he said after the latter inquiry. "You should apologize for asking such a question. Your work is obviously too much for you."

Cohen asked Inspector Lent to return Buckley's card posthumously "as a matter of humanity," but the Inspector quickly denied his request. Two hours into the hearing, Commissioner Kennedy announced the Medical Examiner had found that Lord Buckley died of a long-standing kidney disease, complicated by uremia. Humes and Cohen added that Buckley had eaten virtually nothing in the two days prior to his death.

When the hearing finally ended, Kennedy met with District Attorney Frank Hogan and asked Hogan to grant immunity to entertainers who would testify about licensing pay-offs. Mayor Wagner, meanwhile, ordered Investigation Commissioner Louis Kaplan to investigate the charges of police corruption.

Two days later, Al Wintner, an agent, admitted to having arranged for Buckley to appear at the *Honor Legion* affair, but denied he had ever attempted to intercede to get his performer's card restored or that he even knew a police commissioner. Cohen and Humes were subpoenaed by the

Kaplan investigation, and Humes was later arrested and jailed for outstanding parking tickets.

Cabaret licenses fell into rather immediate disfavor, and in a matter of just a few years were eliminated.

Four days after Richard's death, Clark Gable joined him in eternity. A week before, John F. Kennedy was elected President. Buckley, the man who more than anyone bridged the gap between the two generations those men represented, died midway between the unofficial transfer of idolatry from one to the other.

Theories and rumors swirled throughout the showbiz community concerning his death: "they stuck a nightstick in his kidneys"; "militant blacks poisoned him"; "it was drugs and booze." The most likely explanation, other than the long-term effects of his lifestyle, was somewhat less conspiratorial:

"He died of a broken heart," one friend suggested, "at seeing his big chance go down the drain once more."

The funeral, at the Campbell Mortuary, was attended by some fifty close friends and family. A jazz band played *"America the Beautiful"* – a fitting tribute to a uniquely American performer – and a jazz eulogy recounted His Lordship's magic. One old friend, comedian Sid Gould, while bending over the casket to kiss Lord Buckley on the forehead, slipped a joint into his tux pocket and whispered some last words: "When you get up there Lord, live it up."

His ashes were buried on a mountaintop near his Las Vegas
home.

Praise for the deceased entertainer poured in from all
corners, with longtime friend and supporter Ed Sullivan
perhaps saying it best: "He was a wonderful, decent man.
During the War he was part of my troupe that entertained in
hospitals all over the country. Nobody ever found it
necessary to screen him then or have him carry a police card...

"Sir Laurence Olivier, in "The Entertainer," plays the
part of Archie Rice. The role would have offered even greater
opportunity for Olivier if it had been modelled on *Lord*
Richard Buckley... Buckley was an entertainer known to all in
the profession... Grandiloquent in manner and possessed of
great vitality and authority, he was a 'take charge' performer.
Offstage he was impractical, as many of his profession are,
but the vivid Buckley will long be remembered by all of us."

On December 5th, His friends remembered Lord
Buckley with a rousing memorial, in jazz and jokes, for the
financial benefit of his wife and children, who were left nearly
penniless.

Even as "1000 policemen inspected 2,478 cabarets,
dance halls, and other licensed premises" in massive
retaliation to the cabaret licensing scandal touched off by his
death, Buckley performed his last show, on tape, at the *Jazz
Gallery*.

Many of his famous friends stopped by to pay their respects and perform, including "poets and jazz buffs, musicians and actors, a minister and a midget, and society names." Orson Bean, who said Buckley scolded him "for using stale jokes in Boston" thirteen years earlier, dared the criticism with a string of shaggy dog stories.

Woody Herman dropped by to tell of touring with Richard, and comedian Larry Storch "gained an ounce of revenge for the late Eminence by telling of two gendarmes who had gotten thoroughly inebriated at one of his parties." Gigi Gryce and his group "rolled out a rollicking requiem," and Art Farmer and Benny Golson led their Jazztet in a warm farewell.

Faith Dane brought an oil painting she had done of His Lordship that was to be auctioned off for Lizbeth and the children.

Dizzy Gillespie and Ornette Coleman combined in an attempt "to play five difference tunes all at one time," in Gillespie's words. The effort received a standing ovation.

But the biggest ovation of all was saved for His Highness, heard reciting his translation of *Nero*. The audience was hushed – in respect and concentration.

His voice boomed from the loudspeaker:

"...You just burned down the town last week, Dad, and those cats are unhappy with you..."

The words were still so right, the feeling so alive. It was impossible for many of his friends to believe he was actually gone. They left that night, a piece of their hearts dedicated to the memory of a true original, an incredible performer, and human being.

Lord Buckley was a man "full of so much of the juice of the theater and of life," dedicated to living every moment to the fullest, setting expectations high, and above all, loving.

"We have to spread love," he explained to Studs Terkel two months before his death. "The people of this nation must learn to be more kind, more gracious; must rehearse kindness and graciousness with other people. They must be more generous – the people who have things and are living next door to people who don't have things should give them some of the things they have...

"We have to learn to give more, to tighten and magnetize this nation by love in this coming fight that we're in. We must do it; the government can't do everything. We must help."

Throughout a career that spanned nearly 40 years, Lord Richard Buckley made millions of people laugh, and made millions more think about life and themselves as they never had before. His love for mankind was strong and unfettered; his anger reserved for a world "that can never be as beautiful as we want it to be." Always searching for the perfect Court, he looked deeply into the hearts of his fellow men and saw the future.

He lived hard, loved deeply, and died young. But he never played the blues...

"God Swing 'm and God love 'm."

Author's Notes:

My thanks to all the friends, fans, and showbiz associates of His Lordship for their help and cooperation in researching this biography.

Most especially, to Laurie, Richard and Fred Buckley, and to Lady Lizbeth, who carried the torch of the Royal Court until she split this scene to join her husband on the never-ending Cosmic Tour...

Made in the USA
Columbia, SC
31 October 2022

70244385R00198